Ballade

D1709571

LANGUAGE OF DANCE SERIES

EDITOR
Ann Hutchinson Guest
Director of the Language of Dance Centre
London, UK

ASSOCIATE EDITOR
Ray Cook
Associate Professor, Vassar College
Poughkeepsie, New York, USA

No. 1:
The Flower Festival in Genzano: Pas de Deux
Edited by Ann Hutchinson Guest

No. 2:
Shawn's Fundamentals of Dance
Edited by Ann Hutchinson Guest

No. 3:
Nijinsky's *Faune* Restored
Edited by Ann Hutchinson Guest

No. 4:
Tudor's *Soirée Musicale*
Edited by Ann Hutchinson Guest

No. 5:
***Ballade* by Anna Sokolow**
Compiled by Ray Cook

Other Volumes in Preparation
The First White Ballet from *Robert the Devil*
The Pas de Six from *La Vivandière*
Aureole by Paul Taylor
The Traditional 1870 *Coppélia*

This book is part of a series. The publisher will accept continuation orders which may be cancelled at any time and which provide for automatic billing and shipping of each title in the series upon publication. Please write for details.

Ballade

CHOREOGRAPHY BY

ANNA SOKOLOW

MUSIC BY

ALEXANDER SCRIABIN

TEXT AND LABANOTATION BY

RAY COOK

EDITED BY

ANN HUTCHINSON GUEST

GORDON AND BREACH

Switzerland   Australia   Belgium   France   Germany   Great Britain
India   Japan   Malaysia   Netherlands   Russia   Singapore   USA

Copyright © 1993 by Ray Cook.

Gordon and Breach Science Publishers

Y-Parc
Chemin de la Sallaz
CH-1400 Yverdon
Switzerland

Post Office Box 90
Reading, Berkshire RG1 8JL
United Kingdom

Private Bag 8
Camberwell, Victoria 3124
Australia

3-14-9 Okubo
Shinjuku-ku, Tokyo 169
Japan

58, rue Lhomond
75005 Paris
France

Emmaplein 5
1075 AW Amsterdam
Netherlands

Glinkastrasse 13-15
O-1086 Berlin
Germany

820 Town Center Drive
Langhorne, Pennsylvania 19047
United States of America

Cover Photo: Stanley Love and Elizabeth McPherson dancing in the *Quartet*; a Juilliard Ensemble production.

Photograph of Ray Cook (page xii) by Van Willimas.   By kind permission of the photographer.
Photograph of Anna Sokolow (page xiv) by Doublas R. Long.
Photographs by Oleaga (pages 8, 48, 76, 100).   By kind permission of the photographer.
Photographs by Martha Swope (front cover, pages 30, 70).   By kind permission of the photographer.
Photograph by David Fullard (page 94).   Courtesy of the photographer.
Music: (Opus 11, Nos. 1, 10 & 11; Opus 15, Nos. 2; Opus 32, No. 1; Opus 42, No. 1; Opus 59, No. 2) reproduced by kind permission of Peters Editions Limited, London.

Library of Congress Cataloging-in-Publication-Data

Sokolow, Anna.
      Ballade / choreography, Anna Sokolow ; music by Alexander Scriabin ; text and labanotation by Ray Cook : edited by Ann Hutchinson Guest.
            p.   cm. — (Language of dance series : no. 5)
      Includes index.
      ISBN 2-88124-912-4. — ISBN 2-88124-913-2 (pbk.)
      1. Ballade (Dance)   2. Labanotation.   I. Scriabin, Aleksandr Nikolayevich.   1872–1915.   II. Cook, Ray, 1934–   .   III. Guest, Ann Hutchinson.   IV. Series.
GV1782.62.B35S65   1993
792.8'2—dc20

93-16973
CIP

All rights reserved. Permission for public performance must be obtained in writing from the Players' Project Ltd. No part of this book may be reproduced or utilized in any form or by any means, electronic or mechanical, including photocopying and recording, or by an information storage of retrieval system, without permission in writing from the publishers. Printed in Singapore.

For Anna

both a mentor and a friend

(Photographer unknown. Ray Cook Collection)

CONTENTS

INTRODUCTION TO THE SERIES

The *Language of Dance Series* aims to expand the literature of dance through publication of key works that cover a range of dance styles and dance periods.

A language is spoken, written and read. Those intimately involved in the study and performance of dance will have experienced the language of dance in its "spoken" form, i.e., when it is danced. During the years spent in mastering dance, the component parts are discovered and become part of one's dance language. Through its written form these component parts, the 'building blocks' common to all forms of dance become clear, as well as how these blocks are used. The study of the Language of Dance incorporates these basic elements and the way they are put together to produce choreographic sentences. How the movement sequences are performed, the manner of "uttering" them, rests on the individual's interpretation.

Through careful selection of appropriate movement description, these gems of dance heritage have been translated into Labanotation, the highly developed method of analyzing and recording movement.

In the *Language of Dance Series* understanding of the material is enriched through study and performance notes which provide an aid in exploring the movement sequences and bringing the choreography to life. Whenever possible there is included historical background to place the work in context, and additional information of value to researchers and dance scholars.

Dr. Ann Hutchinson Guest, Editor

FOREWORD

American creative dance is an ethereal art, difficult to grasp, impossible to hold, and, even in this age of telecommunication, inaccessible but to the curious and initiated. It is not elitist, just undiscovered. Less than a century old, American Modern Dance is one of the few original arts that has manifested from the New World. At this moment its legacy is held in the minds and bodies of a few dedicated dancers, rare films and videos found in private or special libraries, unorganized articles and Labanotation. When I was a student at the Boston Conservatory of Music back in the 1960s, there were perhaps a dozen books on the subject. Over the years these libraries have grown, yet much of the history remains undocumented, researched or recognized. Anna Sokolow falls into this category.

This internationally renowned choreographer has been a major influence in the art of dance. However, this past summer when Lorry May and I taught a course on Anna Sokolow at New York University SEHNAP division there was only one book available to the students that dealt specifically with her life, Larry Warren's *Anna Sokolow: The Rebellious Spirit*. Fortunately, as Artistic Director of the Players' Project, Ms. Sokolow's repertory company, I had access to rare documentation to augment this lack of accessible information.

History will prove Anna Sokolow to be one of the most influential choreographers of the twentieth century. *Lyric Suite,* with music by Alban Berg, is essential to any student of choreography; *Rooms* propelled dance into a new era, with the use of jazz, followed over the years by *Evolution of Ragtime* and *Opus 65, Deserts* to music by Varèse. *Magritte, Magritte* has never been equalled in theater/dance; and *Dreams* remains the quintessential expressive dance on humanity, with music by Bach, Webern, and Macero. Ms. Sokolow's recent homage to *Kurt Weill* only verifies her deep understanding of music.

When I first met Anna Sokolow back in 1965 she had just premiered *Opus 65* with the Robert Joffrey Ballet. This shocking work about the alienated and frustrated youth of that era was accentuated by a brilliant, biting jazz score by Teo Macero. The experience of viewing this work was to change forever my concepts about dance. This was the beginning of the post-modern era, and, along with all other arts, dance had become irreverent. It was an exciting, creative time stimulated by originality, especially by Anna Sokolow's choreography.

At the 'old' Juilliard School of Music one day, I passed a dance studio, from which the music of Alexander Scriabin was emanating. This was a time of revolt! Romantic, passionate music was something to be avoided at all costs. Yet my sensitive side compelled me to listen, which led me to peer into the studio. There in the middle of the studio was the fearless leader of the rebellion, Anna Sokolow, demonstrating a deeply beautiful, lyrical movement. In the midst of the post-modern movement Anna Sokolow decided to choreograph to Scriabin. This was typically daring and a complete switch from her previous works. *Ballade* proved to be a very classical dance, yet curiously modern. The movement phrasing and the music became one.

Ballade has been incorporated into the Players' Project repertory, with the addition of the male solo, and has been performed in Europe, the Far East, Mexico, and throughout the United States. This popular work shows Anna Sokolow's versatility of style and dispels that popular belief that she is the choreographer of doom and gloom. *Ballade* illustrates rather that she is, also, a poet-choreographer. Anna Sokolow's legacy remains as one of the thriving forces in dance, not only in America, but around the world.

The importance of notating her work has been almost single-handedly accomplished by Ray Cook. As an early member of Anna's company, he was the perfect person to record *Rooms*. Over the years Mr. Cook has penned many of her works, has taught throughout the world her unique approach to dance and theater, is considered a personal friend to Ms. Sokolow, and is recognised as one of the few authorities of her style. This book is one more treasured gift to the future, to society, and especially to the students of dance.

Jim May, Artistic Director
Player's Project

(Van Williams)

Ray Cook performing in his choreography *Land of Tears*.

ACKNOWLEDGEMENTS

I wish to express my appreciation to all who have contributed to this book. Anna Sokolow made available her collection of reviews and programs, which along with material from the Lincoln Center Dance Collection, the Young Men and Young Women's Hebrew Association at 92nd Street (the YM-YWHA), The Juilliard School and the Dance Notation Bureau all in New York City, provided information for the chronology. Larry Warren, author of Sokolow's biography was most helpful in contributing to and in checking the accuracy of my chronology.

Sections of the score were given practical trial through use in a course on Directing from the Score, given by the Dance Notation Bureau in New York City; by Dr. Jill Beck's class at The Juilliard School, and by Tom Brown's notation students at the 1990 Fifth Hong Kong International Dance Conference/Festival.

My thanks go to Vassar College for the grant given toward preparation of this publication.

The beautiful Labanotation autography is by Irene Politis.

My thanks are extended to Jane Dulieu for final camera-ready-copy, and to Ann Hutchinson Guest for her enthusiasm for the project and help in bringing it to fruition.

(Douglas R. Long)

Anna Sokolow rehearsing in a New York City studio.

PERSONAL REMINISCENCES OF ANNA SOKOLOW

"Emotion creates motion."

How best can I introduce Anna Sokolow to you? There must be a hundred stories I could tell. Anna, born of Russian immigrants, growing up on the Lower East side of Manhattan; Anna taking dancing lessons against her parents' wishes, *"You'd be no more than a whore",* her mother told her; the richest man in Mexico wanting Anna for his paramour; Anna striking a dancer to get the result she wanted; Anna winning her case and tearing up an out-of-court settlement check from Joseph Papp or Anna sponsoring talented dancers from overseas. But these would all be second-hand stories. I prefer to share my memories of times which I spent with Anna, memories that will shed light on how she works and give some idea of the sources of her inspiration.

I first met Anna Sokolow in 1963 when I was a student at the Juilliard Dance Division in New York City. Anna was choreographing a new ballet, *Opus 63*. It was a large cast, as she loved to give as many students as possible the opportunity to work with her. A special weekend rehearsal was called for the nine men in the 'twist section'. Only four turned up. I was terrified because now there was nobody to hide behind. I was a ballet dancer and did not know how to twist or improvise. Anna was upset and I was determined not to upset her still further. She kept calling for more, more, more. I did not have a clue as to what she wanted so I just 'went crazy'. She loved it. What had I done? Through the years I was to see this pattern repeated over and over again. Anna made all her dancers go beyond their limits, to be always in competition with themselves. She was never satisfied. The end result was that when you went on stage you were not dancing something that felt comfortable and easy. On stage you still strove to give her more. There was always a dangerous edge to what you did.

The following year I was given the drumming solo in *Dreams*, her choreographic indictment of Nazi Germany. In silence I sat on the stool. Two pieces of wood held in my hands acted as imaginary drum sticks. I began to imagine what it must have been like to be a young drummer in a band before being thrown into a concentration camp. I started to lift the sticks. A quiet voice said, *"I don't believe you".* For the entire rehearsal I did not raise the sticks above shoulder height. *"I don't believe you. I don't believe you."* The next day was the same. As I brought them down onto an imaginary drum, she still did not believe me.

That night I decided to quit dancing and wrote her a letter. Two days later I had what was for me a revelation. My weakness as a performer had nothing to do with dance technique, it was acting. I returned, and began to understand this woman's very personal way of working. Although I did not know it then, *Dreams* had been first choreographed on her drama students at the H. Bergdorf Acting Studio in New York City, the studio where I soon went for acting classes and where she still teaches today.

Year after year I observed Anna rehearse new groups of young dancers at the Juilliard Dance Division. As I watched them struggle to give what she demanded she would turn to me and say, *"They just don't understand my way of working, nobody else works like this, it is important for them to know how to work"*. Understudies and visitors who came to watch were often brought to tears as she coached her dancers, inspiring them with devastating and yet beautiful images.

How can this seemingly fragile woman of five-feet-two coax the performances she does out of her dancers, and often dancers with little classroom technique? I have witnessed her going up to the strongest man in a company with his arms outstretched and force them down. She requires a high use of raw energy. She wants to **see** the energy, to see how difficult it is to perform a phrase of movement, and she is **never** satisfied.

One look from her was enough to know that you could give more. When we were told that we were migrating birds and **had** to get through that imaginary brick wall we hurled ourselves, rebounded, fell, clambered up and tried again and again to smash through. As she choreographed, image after image was fed to us; like a bird **trying** to fly; walk with the footsteps of a Gestapo on the stone pavement; a shadow is passing over you, look and there is no one there; you are like a sand dune continually changing shape; first the hunter and now the hunted; explode like an atomic blast; you are a faceless soldier, march!; your kiss is 'the kiss of Judas'; you sway because the earth sways beneath you; struggle like a man buried alive, and so on. She was never at a loss for images.

Sokolow's choreographic subject matter may best be summarized by repeating part of a conversation I heard on a taxi ride through Central Park in the early '60's. Anna was explaining to José Limón that whereas she danced about the piles of garbage seen around us everyday, José danced about the single flower that bloomed on top of that pile. This truism is evident in such dances as *Steps of Silence*, *Dreams*, *Rooms*. Anna has often said, *"Hell, what is there to be happy about?"*

One Sunday, after a rehearsal of *Steps of Silence*, we were walking through Union Square and saw a homeless person covered with newspaper lying in the doorway of a Chase Manhattan bank. Church bells began to chime. *"There,"* she said, grabbing my arm, *"people think I'm crazy, but I'm not."* She was referring to the final image in her choreography for *Steps of Silence* in which near-naked men and women lie twitching in a pile of wind-blown newspapers while bells chime in the distance.

On many a summer's evening after dinner together in an East Village restaurant she would take me for a long, winding walk through the streets, pointing out the everyday landmarks where she had spent her childhood and the scenes through open windows. It was, of course, these scenes through open windows that had inspired her to choreograph *Rooms*. She had seen young girls leaning on their window sills, day-dreaming on a hot summer evening; heard the mournful sound of a lonely trumpet in a distant room; looked into a young man's room to see walls were plastered with his idols; noticed a plain-looking girl who was waiting for a lover who would never come and felt the terror of a lonely corridor in a tenement building with only a dim naked light burning. In her choreography for *Rooms* all this came to life for us.

Anna has always enjoyed eating out. Almost every night will find her dining with a friend, sometimes a famous actor, composer or dancer, sometimes one of her students. Whenever we have dined together there has always been someone, often many, who came up to her on the street. *"Anna, you don't remember me but I danced in so and so."* A friendly conversation would follow, hugs and kisses and then the goodbye. Sometimes Anna would remember but so often she would turn to me and say that she had no idea who that person was. No, this was not being rude. Anna has worked with thousands of professional dancers and actors all over the world. Nobody forgets Anna Sokolow.

This woman can make a lion out of a mouse; she destroys you in rehearsals only to build you up again from the bottom by making you realize you have potentials you never dreamed existed. One evening at a Juilliard concert, a young dancer received bravos from the audience. I remarked on what a wonderful dancer this young woman was. *"Do you know"*, Anna said, *"that she cried at every rehearsal, saying that she could not do it?"*

In the mid-60's we were rehearsing at the old Clark Center which was in the YWCA at 8th Avenue and 51st Street in New York City. I don't remember the dance but Anna was demanding more of us. *"More - More - More!"* she demanded until one dancer, Clyde Morgan, a six-foot-two black member of our company stopped and asked, *"More what Anna? I'm already giving blood."* The whole room froze. Nobody ever questioned Anna Sokolow. We were all sent out of the room except Clyde and the door was shut behind us. Half an hour later one member of the company thought he had better knock on the door and enquire what was to be done. To our surprise and relief Anna and Clyde were enjoying a cigarette together and were smiling from ear to ear. We don't know to this day what was said. With her intense way of working Anna can intimidate people, whereas, in truth, she is the most approachable, accessible and helpful person I know.

Another memory comes from being on tour somewhere in the hinterlands. At one particular college Anna had agreed to spend several hours choreographing for the students to give them the experience of working with a professional. At this particular rehearsal one of the men just did not understand what was required of him. Like a drill sergeant Anna delivered instructions. Do this, do that, she cried, and finally turning to me, winked, and with all seriousness took up a metal paper bin and hurled it across the room. Pick it up. He did. Bring it here. He did. Put it down there. He did. Go back to the group. He did. I remember this well for two reasons. Firstly, Anna never winked, and secondly, it showed the power that choreographers have over their dancers. Like that young man we never spoke during rehearsals and we never sat down. We were never late and we never questioned. Visiting dancers from other companies and other countries would often comment after watching a rehearsal that they could not believe how we just stood and waited in silence for our next instruction.

Dancers will do anything a choreographer asks. We bruised our bodies and often bled trying to give her what she wanted. Much of Anna's choreography has sections of unplanned running and leaping. We listened in silence as we were given the image of what should happen and then we performed. Yes, fully performed; you never indicated or marked in her rehearsals, for to mark meant that the movements were from another dance. Energy, quality and phrasing demanded more attention than did the actual steps. She knew that if we planned our paths and knew in advance where we were going, the spontaneity would be lost. In reproducing her works, it is this look of spontaneity that is most difficult to achieve because dancers want to know exactly where they are expected to be on stage. Whenever one of us would begin to offer a suggestion, a finger was quickly raised followed by a brief *"uh-uh"* that made it clear who was in charge.

Anna does not read music or play an instrument yet she is one of our most musical choreographers. Unlike Balanchine she does not slavishly follow the musical rhythms. She choreographs more in the vein of Tudor, where the choreography has its own musical phrasing which flows through the music. Hers is so individualistic that it is immediately recognizable as Sokolow phrasing. Many times we worked with her in silence on a dance phrase that was over a minute in length. When she felt it was phrased correctly the music was put on. As the section of music came to an end the dance phrase would inevitably also come to an end. This is a rare gift and shows her deep feeling and understanding of music.

Every day at 81, Anna can be found teaching somewhere in New York City. In a choreography class I watched at Mary Anthony's Dance Studio she told her students to devour more music than food. Her love of music is broad as can be witnessed by the concerts she attends and her record collection. Her apartment is full of gifts from her grateful and loving students from around the world. There is not one clear area of wall or shelf space anywhere. Paintings, sketches, wall hangings, plaques, sculpture, books, records and fresh flowers adorn this woman's apartment in the West Village. Many books are dog-eared with re-reading. And what of her reading preferences? Her favorite form is biography. She has told me many times how inspiring it is for her to read the lives of the world's great artists. Some of these biographies have resulted in new dances, *Steps of Silence*, for example, was inspired by Solzhenitsyn. She goes to the best of plays and the latest of plays and will not hesitate to walk out if the directing and acting do measure up to her standards. She knows that you cannot have honest words coming from a dishonest body, something too prevalent in the theater.

Her *Ballade* came upon the dance world like a spring shower - fresh, joyful, youthful and passionate. In its sweep across the stage it became the forerunner of such notable works as *Dancers at a Gathering* by Jerome Robbins. But even in this dance, in the final moments, she cannot help but show us the pain that can be part of passionate love. She once asked a student in a choreography class, *"Who are you leaving? What are you leaving? How do you feel about leaving?"* She told the student that her accents were too predictable. The pain was too easy and that her rhythm was not the rhythm of pain.

Anna Sokolow has been described as a romantic classicist with a sharply developed sense of social consciousness who speaks out on today, a difficult task master, tough and outspoken, the mistress of doom and gloom, impatient, generous, helpful, enormously stimulating and always true to herself; but I prefer most of all what her Mexican dancers said of her, *"She is a rebel, but with discipline"*.

Ray Cook

NOTES ON DIRECTING *BALLADE*

Each of Scriabin's pieces selected for this work is a perfectly spun miniature. Because of the brevity of each section the dancers have little time to capture the ever-changing mood. There is no time for them to build to each new mood. Thus preparation must be achieved in the wings so that the change in mood is brought onto the stage 'with the music'. The dancers must commence each section completely involved.

The movement behind the steps and the phrasing of the music must be individually discovered. The steps as such and the musical counts are of less importance.

The embraces and touchings are sensitive and undecorative. Do not worry if the dancers cannot arrive at some of the exact shapes written. Find the intention behind the movement - because of different heights the dancers may end in a slightly different embrace: the intention, mood and timing are the most important aspects of the dance. The audience must not be aware of any technique.

All arm movements emanate from the back and occur only because they have been motivated from within. The simpler the better - mannerisms must be avoided. All runs are performed with chest opened wide and a forward projection. This is not written in the score.

If the size of the stage makes the paths for exiting difficult they may be altered slightly. In no cases should the exits or traffic, the coming and going look planned. The use of space must look spontaneous; in fact the entire dance should be so well rehearsed that the overriding image received by the audience is that of spontaneous emotion amongst young lovers. (This is particularly true in the very fast sections.)

Transitions need as much work as the actual 'steps'. The phrases do not just start, each emerges from the previous phrase. Transitions should make what follows look inevitable.

THE INDIVIDUAL DANCES

Opening

The mood here must be established at once, otherwise there is no reason for what follows - the spontaneous meetings of lovers. They sweep across the stage, 'run through the woods', to meet the loved one. As the number of dancers increases, momentum builds ending in a burst of passion, an embrace. It is important to be aware of which phrases have free timing and those for which specific timing is stated.

Opening Continued

In this brief section which follows the entrances, the chest should always be held open and 'projected'. The weight should be carried high in the body. This carriage is true of the entire dance but especially so in the fast sections.

Quartet

The motivation for this section is remembrances. In measures 21-24 do not try to set the men's movement. Set the intention and smooth out the movement later. The men may have to vary the tempo of their walk as they circle the women. All walking patterns that end in a rendezvous are to be walked exactly on the beat as notated. However, in some instances, depending on the size of the stage, dancers often need to walk through the ritardando. In all such instances maintain the same tempo as that of the previous movement so the walking remains flowing and rhythmical.

Woman's Solo

The entrance of the solo woman concludes the previous section. Enter anticipating a meeting with your lover but he is not there. What follows is a quiet personal moment alone. Finally your lover arrives.

Poem: Two Duets

The timing of walks must be exactly as written. All *cabrioles* in which the torso is lying back must be done in a strict two, not in a three which is more usual. You must set your own images as you cross and recross the stage. The phrase builds in excitement because of the insistence of the same step, the traveling *cabriole*.

Man's Solo

This solo is based on images of Nijinsky although, obviously, it is not danced balletically. Some images, such as those of the faun on his rock, *Les Orientales* and *Narcissus* looking at his reflection in the water, are quite obvious. This entire solo needs to be performed with the sensuality of a magnificent animal.

Ending

Lovers' quarrel - the lovers who were so close are now far apart; hurling throwing - pulling with highest energy - every moment pushed to agonizing limits. The dance ends with each dancer searching for his or her lover, yet sometimes reaching out to no one.

PRODUCTION NOTES

Casting

All dancers should be youthful and capable of a wide range of movement qualities resulting from emotional qualities.

In the Opening the women must be capable of high and free *grands jetés en tournants* performed with a high arched chest.

The Woman's Solo requires a dancer with a face that is alive and alert. A high *attitude* on *relevé* and an arched chest is also required.

For the Man's Solo an animal quality is needed to bring the images to life. A good jump is also required.

For the Ending the women dancers should not be afraid to throw themselves into the movement and into the floor.

Costumes

In the original production the men wore beige-colored short-sleeved shirts with an open V-neck. These were tucked in at the waist, their trousers were brown with a slight flare at the bottom. Modern dance sandals were worn.

The women wore knee-length dresses with a scooped neck line. The sleeves were tight-fitting and reached half-way to the elbows. One dress was pink, one was orange. Over each dress the women wore layers of chiffon in the same color as the dress. In each the color bleeds from one shade to another. The bottom layer of chiffon was ragged-looking and longer in length than the dress. Modern dance sandals were worn. In later productions soft, flesh-colored ballet shoes have been worn.

Curtain

The curtain opens quickly on the first four measures of music. It closes at a moderate speed after the music has ended and while the dancers are still dancing.

Lights

The stage is filled with bright sunlight for the entire ballet. The lights may be dimmed or faded up for some of the sections. All light changes must be unobtrusive.

If there is no curtain the lights swell during the first four introductory measures. At the end of the dance they commence fading during the last few measures of music and continue through the silence to a complete blackout.

8

Opening, meas. 14
The preparation for the 'throw'.
Eric Hampton and Tamara Woshokiwska dancing in the original production.

(Oleaga)

STUDY AND PERFORMANCE NOTES

Opening

[1-2]   During the first three measures the curtain quickly rises.   The music played *vivace* is building to a *crescendo* which will sweep the lovers across the stage.

[3-11]   K, the first dancer to enter, rises (a slow *relevé*) in the wings in preparation for the run that will sweep him across the stage from stage right to stage left.   Before he has time to exit, H, a woman, runs similarly from upstage left to downstage right only to be met by another man P, who has just entered from downstage right to 'catch' her in his left arm.   After a brief moment of suspension they both run upstage to exit where she first entered.   When they are center stage, the last of the four dancers, W (a woman), enters downstage left and runs around the stage exiting upstage left after the couple.

[12-15]   Immediately the first couple re-enters with P running backwards and holding H's hands, leading her onto the stage.   A brief pause.   A mood of exhilarating young love has been set.   Still holding hands, both *chassé* down on the same diagonal line.   In a moment of ecstasy the woman does a *grand jeté en tournant*, chest arched backwards and focus to the sky.   She is lifted high by the man throwing her into the air.   As she passes downstage of him he turns to keep her in front of him.   He then passes downstage of her in a low *grand jeté en tournant*.   As the woman turns to face him they are again in their original position ready to repeat the *chassé* and *grand jeté en tournant* sequence [16,17].   Meanwhile the second couple (W and K) have entered dancing this same sequence but one count later.

[17-21]   The last phrase is ended as H quickly *piqués* to a 1st position on half-toe, turning a half to end at the left side of her partner P who has *relevéd* in place.   Both are now facing upstage left, arm around the other's waist, their chests arched left diagonally backward, anticipating the direction into which they will next circle.   One beat behind them, the second couple do likewise, adjusting so that both end facing downstage right.   The phrase climaxes with each couple doing three 'coupé piqués' backward in unison on the inside foot as they make a half circle anticlockwise.   The phrase ends in a stylised 4th position *plié*, the outside leg having opened sideward before coming down to the back to take weight on a forced arch. The torso is now rounded forward and parallel to the ground.   The men take two undercurving forward steps away from their partners, at the same time each woman reaches her right arm forward to take her partner's left hand, turning her head to lay her right cheek on his hand - a tender moment.

[22]   All dancers now retrace their path moving backward on the diagonal doing the same step pattern but in an unpredictable canon; the timing for each dancer being different.   Some commence quickly and slow down, others do the phrase very quickly.   Sometimes one moves

alone and sometimes two commence at the same time.[1] The overall image should be of spontaneous outbursts of passion reaching back to where they were, or to their partner if they are in front of them. The phrase is a low turning spring backwards into a large 4th position lunge; the weight does not rise during the spring. The arms pull backward when landing in the 4th position lunge and then release the pull backward into a forward pull being guided by the upper arm. As the arms swing through the torso rounds forward and then 'rolls' out sequentially as the arms reach forward. The focus is down on the lunge and forward with the reach of the arms.

[26-27] The next phrase is in unison and offers a contrast to the one just performed. All dancers, having ended in a lunge with the right foot back, then spiral the torso, inclining it as they twist around to the left, and looking behind them to the left back diagonal. The spiral then releases into a vertical position arching round to the right. This is accompanied by a half-turn rise to half-toe on the left leg, the right leg ending gesturing forward. A sink into a 4th position *plié* follows with the torso spiralling to the right.

[27-31] The half-turn is now reversed; the body coming upright and untwisted leads into a quick adjusting step so that the partners end once again side by side as before, arms again around the partner's waist. The *piqué* step backwards is now repeated six times, each pair revolving once to the left as they travel on a straight path to the upstage right corner. Each couple ends by adjusting into the relationship in which they first started their duets, but now the man faces upstage right with the woman facing him.

[32-38] After a slight concentrated pause the opening diagonal phrase is repeated in unison. This time the phrase ends with the dancers changing their relationship. Each couple faces front with the man behind the woman, his right arm passionately wrapped around her waist, having pulled her in toward him. As the music climaxes each dancer does a head roll in a slow circle in any direction; this is then repeated much faster. This section ends with a very quick spontaneous rush into the tightest of groups, some facing towards a center, others in any direction, with arms in various forms of rapturous group embrace. Each dancer has a different focus and weight distribution.

Opening Continued

This next section is choreographed with the type of phrases that can never be done quickly enough or with enough high energy to satisfy the choreographer. It commences at the level of intensity with which the first section ended and continues to build until [35]. There is an alertness to the steps which is suggestive of birds or animals listening to unfamiliar sounds. This is especially true in the running phrases which end in a high 4th position.

[1-4] With arms by their sides, all four dancers *chaîné* at their fastest speed to any position on the stage that is far from the downstage left corner. They end facing into any direction. The

---

[1] This is a device commonly used by the choreographer. A phrase is set and then passed from one dancer to another in an unpredictable sequence and rhythm.

first *chaîné* commences with a low *chassé* step to the side that is strongly emphasized, almost like 'digging' into the floor.[2] The *chaînés* end in an uplifted, buoyant high 4th position.

[4-7] This unison phrase [1-3] is followed by a 'broken' phrase [4-7] during which the dancers create their own phrases based on the previous one. They now make three or four brief runs, again ending in the high 4th position. Sometimes a knee is swiftly lifted high to 'stab' the ground as they take the 4th position.[3]

[8] Everybody holds - alert.

[9-14] Commencing at [9] the dancers catch the pulse in the music and count the next phrase.[4] With chest arched and focus high, each dancer does a step-hop in low *arabesque* on the right foot, followed by a *piqué* to *arabesque* on the left foot, turning three-quarters of a turn to give the dancer the maximum degree of directional change. This is followed by two *chaîné* turns. Like wings, the arms are lifted to the side in the *sauté* and brought quickly down during the *piqué* turn, remaining there during the *chaînés*. The above phrase is done in canon by each dancer commencing one beat after the other. H starts, first followed by P, W and K.

[15-16] By [14] all except K have exited. K completes the phrase with a final step-hop and a run in a half-circle, counterclockwise, to end almost center stage. He ends facing the audience in a high 1st position. He now 'winds' himself up with a chest spiral to the left, his right arm crossing low and in front of the body.

[17-18] The music now having a retard, he slowly 'unwinds' to end facing stage right stepping into a long lunge on the right leg, the torso leaning forward as the slightly curved right arm indicates the direction into which he will next travel; his left arm is back in opposition to the right. The dancer should pull this phrase out as long as he can before releasing into a big leap to the right which ends with a very quick turn. During the leap his chest arches diagonally back right to give the effect of leaning backward into the turn. The right arm sweeps upward to help the dancer gain the greatest possible height. The full turn in *plié* that follows the leap serves as a quick recovery.

[19-20] The phrase of [17-18] is repeated.

[21-33] As K exits stage right, two of the other three dancers re-enter each doing material from the previous exiting phrase. P enters from upstage left running like the wind, arms sideward and exits downstage right with a *grand jeté*, chest arched backwards. As P is about to exit, W enters from upstage right and circles clockwise to downstage left performing three times the exiting step pattern. This is followed with the short 'broken' phrase of [4-7], during

---

[2] This, again, is typical of the choreographer's work. Such strong emphasis given to a movement that is usually performed otherwise gives the dancers a pulse which fills the stage with high energy.

[3] Whenever the choreographer has these fast phrases with some freedom for the dancers, she always emphasizes the moments of stillness. The holding is just as important as the moving. Held with a high intensity, it is the holds which give the unpredictable rhythms to the choreography.

[4] Counting is very untypical of the choreographer but in such quick phrases done in canon it becomes necessary.

which she must be sure to stay in the upstage left area of the stage. She may end facing in any direction. H enters downstage left after W has completed one phrase of step-hop, *piqué*, *chaîné*. She does the same step as W [24,25] and then runs across stage ending with a *grand jeté*. She now joins W in the 'broken' phrase being sure to stay in the downstage right area of the stage. H also ends facing any stage direction. K runs in from upstage right, performs a *grand jeté*, then runs again before joining in the 'broken' phrase. P now re-enters from where he exited with the same run and leap as he did on his last crossing. He joins the other three dancers in the 'broken' phrase being sure to stay in the right upstage area of the stage. P also ends facing in any stage direction. All four dancers are now spread around the stage.

[33-35] Having all danced the 'broken' phrase, they come to a brief and energy-filled pause. All dancers now *chaîné*, arms down, ending in various positions of alertness, all arms remaining down. W and H *chaîné* towards upstage left while P and K *chaîné* towards downstage left. K ends facing stage right, H faces front, W and P downstage left. The dancers should now be positioned on the stage to suggest remoteness from one another.[5]

Quartet

The music is 6/8 at a moderate tempo, melodic and continually flowing. Moving with it, the dancers use this flow and the on-goingness of the music to help sweep them around the stage to the chance meetings that lovers sometimes have. In this section, as in all of the dance, the movement is simple and undecorated.

[1-4] The dancers hold the end pose from the previous section and listen to the music, recalling the past. Towards the end of the first measure they breath in and suspend before doing the quickest of catch steps to face into the direction in which they will walk. Dancer K faces stage right, W the audience, P downstage right, and H upstage. These facing enable the dancers to move out and to cover as much of the stage as possible. With weight carried high in the body and arms by their sides, the dancers sweep through the space (a forest perhaps?), each looking for his/her lover. The paths are large curves during which the chest arches slightly back over one shoulder, leaning towards the center of the circle being traveled. The section ends with W downstage center and with K coming in behind her gently to take her downstage hand with his upstage hand. This causes her to pause and slowly turn her head to the left to see who it is. P has not met anyone and has ended alone in the upstage right area, facing the corner. He slowly turns his head, as if remembering a moment similar to that being experienced by K and W. This turn of his head leads into a slow half-turn at the end of which he is looking directly at H.[6] H's final path finishes straight down the center stage ending behind K and W. She looks out past them as if they do not exist. She is looking for her lover, P. Except for the slow turning of the dancer's head the stage image has come to rest.

---

[5] Note that the choreographer has stayed with the thematic material and manipulated it simply by changing directions and facings on stage. On the final re-entrances in this section, the dancers commence with longer paths which become shorter and with more directional changes. These short, and abrupt phrases then make one final statement uniting the dancers as they move in unison but to different areas of the stage.

[6] This is a choreographic device used by many choreographers in which the audience sees what the performer is 'seeing' even when the performer doesn't actually see it.

[5-6]   Again the quick upbeat catch step and all walk new but similar paths coming again to rest in a beautiful stage picture.

[7-8]   This time K and W have finished upstage center, an arm's length apart and both facing stage right. W's concluding steps have been backward. She did not see K. K places his right hand forward onto the back of W's head to stop her. He gently turns it to the left thus motivating a half-pivot turn on her left foot accompanied by a slight lowering and rounding of the torso. She ends facing K bowed forward towards him. This turn leads into a full circular head motion, rolling to the left. As the head continues its roll she increases the depth of her knee bend. This very simple phrase should appear as if, with his hand, the man is leading the woman through her movements. At the same time, as if by accident, H and P have met stage right toward downstage. P has closed in behind H and ends with his body gently touching hers, their hands touching. He quietly presses her arms to her side. The sensation of him touching her causes her head to arch to the right, this in turn leads into a *plié* on her right foot as her left leg traces an outward circle on the floor. She ends this circle with the feeling that her leg is 'wrapped' around P's left leg and as though her body is moulded to his, her body arching slightly backwards and to the right. Her right arm now reaches around to the right and embraces his right leg from behind. As she reaches around she turns her head to the left to look up at him. The phrase ends as he kisses her neck, an inevitable result.[7]

[9]   The mood is broken. Each of the women now leaves her man and the men then go in search of them. The first to break away is W who looks into K's face and places her right hand on K's right shoulder. She reacts by stepping forward on her right foot and rises into a low *arabesque*, chest arched backward. She turns away from K and commences a low leaping phrase changing from left to right with no transitional steps in between. With arms rounded sideward and rotated outward, chest still arched and focus high, she covers as much space as possible through the next three steps.

W: [10-15]   She continues traveling in a combination of long curved and straight paths. In [13] the smooth regular leaping phrase becomes a broken one with large leaps during which the dancer may run in between the leaps but must hold each landing for a few beats.

K: [9-13]   As W leaves, K lowers his right arm but maintains his body shape. The effect is as if one half of a piece of sculpture has left while the other half remains. After a few leaps by W, K suspends as he rises, arches his chest backwards, and, with arms held side low, picks up the same leaping phrases as W as he searches the stage for her. He commences the broken phrase at the same moment as W. His overall path must be distant from that of W. H and P perform a similar type of parting, followed by the same regular leaping phrase. H leaves on [10] and P follows on [11].[8]

---

[7] Both of the above phrases are very typical Sokolow phrases. Each movement leads into the next. There must be no 'seams' or visible transitions. The sensation of a touch makes the following movements inevitable. These are the types of phrases that the choreographer will spend hours rehearsing. Seemingly simple, they must never look planned or rehearsed. The director is encouraged to take the motivation and allow the movements to evolve. Because of body heights, the final embrace and poses may end slightly differently.

[8] The overall image will be one of accumulation, another Sokolow choreographic device, i.e. each of the dancers commences a phrase one after the other until the stage is filled with dancers all doing the same movement pattern but not necessarily in unison.

[15] At [15] all dancers direct their leaping phrase towards the upstage right area of the stage ending facing downstage left, feet in 1st position, high level, arms out to the sides. The phrase now becomes unison movement with the group sweeping through the music in a brief final run into a small group in the downstage left area.

[17-18] The phrase climaxes as the men, first P and then K, quickly turn to face their woman, lunging far forward towards them, and, with outstretched arm, grasp their partner's hand and whip them in towards themselves. Commencing with a lunge on the left foot, the women do the fastest of *chaînés*. They do one full turn plus any adjusting needed to end wrapped in their man's arm. All end facing the audience. This is an abrupt ending to all that has gone before.[9]

[18] K and P turn in to face what will be the center of a circle. They are opposite one another and in a 4th position backward lunge, the right foot being back in a *plié* on a forced arch. With a slight contraction their arms reach out to the side and take the hands of the women who, having adjusted into the spaces between them, are in a position similar to the men. All four dancers have formed an enclosed circle.

[19-20] The group now commences a counterclockwise circle, stepping first on the right foot. They mark out the rhythm, (2-4-5) and then continue [20] to step on every beat. They let go hands [21] and continue as couples, W and K being one couple, P and H the other. Each couple continues to turn.

[21-23] Couple K and W now travel upstage to end in upstage left corner. At the start W lowers her arms while K's arms reach out as if to embrace her. She continues to revolve on a straight path while he circles around her. Couple H and P do likewise ending in the upstage right corner. As the phrase concludes each couple adjusts to end in new relationships. W and P face one another, W facing stage right. Their downstage hands reach out and touch while their chests turn toward the audience. Both look down towards their hands. (In this pose K will appear to be whispering to W when they start to walk forward.) They are alone. Far from them, and also alone, the other couple have ended facing the audience, P's hands on H's shoulders. P who is at the right of H lets go of her shoulders and turns his chest to address her as he wraps his left arm around her chest. She lays her head on her partner's left shoulder and places her right hand behind his head.

[25-30] All dancers walk to the front of the stage taking six steps.[10] H and P take forward steps while W and K take sideward steps toward the front of the stage. Couple P and H both start on the right foot, stepping on the first and fourth beats of the measure. K and W

---

[9] The previous leaping phrase, and almost all that are constructed in this way, are shaped by the dancers. For dancers who have worked together for a long time there is a sensitivity and awareness that allows them to take the choreographer's instructions and shape a phrase. This is particularly true regarding timing and spacing. For example, in this free leaping phrase the performers become aware of another dancer's directional change even before it occurs and know that they must go into another area of the stage, thus fulfilling the choreographer's instruction to fill the stage. When the broken leaping phrase occurs they know not to leap and hold at the same time as another dancer. The individual dancer begins to sense who may take the initiative for starting the changes and who will follow. Of course the final decision rests in the hands of the choreographer who may wish the movements to be done exactly as previously or she may prefer to shape further what the dancers have established. A good memory is therefore required.

[10] This phrase, though involving only simple walking, is typical of one on which the choreographer will spend many hours in rehearsal.

start on the downstage foot stepping on the third and sixth beats of the measure. It is very important that each step must be performed exactly on the beat and be clipped enough to finish a breath before the other dancer takes the next step. Each step must look as if it is motivated by the previous step of the other couple. On the last beat each dancer releases any contact and, with the same quick upbeat catch step used in [1], commence the walking paths with which the dance first started. The paths they perform now will be different as each dancer curves through the space but they end as they did in [4].

[31-36] The next two measures are a repeat of the walking in [5-6]. Continuing with this repeat, the dancers perform the movement of [7-8], however this time they stretch it out to cover four measures coming to a cadence with the music, [33-36].

[37-39] Now comes another parting. W is the first to leave. She rises in a low *arabesque* turning to face the audience and runs in a circular path to exit downstage right. With his right arm, K, her partner, gestures after her. Why is she leaving? He runs after her, following her, pauses for a moment downstage to watch her disappear and then follows her off. The third dancer to leave is H who rises in 1st and pivots to face stage left. In contrast to the two previous dancers, her exit is on a direct path to downstage left. Her partner P rises slightly later and pivots in the opposite direction, circling briefly clockwise before following her on a parallel path exiting stage left.

[39] As the stage empties, W enters again on the last note of the music from the far upstage right wing. She has returned to look for her lover. All is quiet. She looks toward downstage left. She realizes she is alone.[11]

The next dance is a solo and offers a contrast, a moment of solitude.

Woman's Solo

[1] The music for this solo is in 6/8, the dancer's counts being one count for each 1/8 (quaver) note. During the silence before the music starts the dancer W takes a slow deep breath rising lightly onto the forced arch. She *tombés* forward into a long lunge on the right foot rolling through the foot to make the step smooth and very controlled. The torso leans forward while her focus remains into the downstage left corner where her lover may be. She then 'flings' her arms forward, leading with the elbows and allowing the arms to rotate inward. The back of the wrists end almost touching. With the same intensity as the fling she bends the arms slightly, ending with the hands pointing upward and the palms toward one another. Her arms slowly bend until the wrists are beneath her chin, her face being framed by her hands. Her weight has shifted slightly backwards. Her face projects forward, and she is beautiful.

[2] The first beat of the measure is held. She shifts her weight backwards onto her left foot in *plié*. Her torso, rounded over the front, tilts forward parallel to the floor. Her pelvis is

---

[11] By now the reader may have noticed another Sokolow choreographic preference. When covering a lot of space the movement is simple and repetitive, walks, runs, *chassés* and simple leaps. When the dancers pause, and particularly when in couples, the movement is more complex and very sculptured.

'tucked' under making a long rounded torso.   At the same time her arms have melted downwards. She now rolls backward through the torso making the longest line from her right foot to her head while her arms rise sequentially to side high. The phrase ends with a quick rise on the left foot, the right leg lifting forward high, the torso vertical, chest arched backwards, head parallel to the floor. The movement on the last beat acts as a transition into the next movement.

[3] Her chest spirals to the right and continues to arch backward over her right shoulder while her rounded right arm lifts high to assist the uplift that is needed to place the right foot back in a 4th position. She pivots a half-turn, sinking into a 4th position *plié* with the left foot on a forced arch. Her torso now completes the line started by the chest. As she *pliés*, her right arm lowers, led by the elbow, ending rounded. She looks down towards her right hand. She holds. She reverses this rise and turns to end in 4th *plié* with the previous body arch now on the other side. Then, as a quick upbeat into the new movement in the next measure, pivots to the right a full turn on her left foot. Her right leg is now extended low in front, her chest again arching to the right back diagonal. She ends facing downstage left.

[4] Coming upright with her arm lifted sidewards, rounded and rotated outwards, she *chassés* forward with the right foot as a preparation into a series of *enchaîné* turns, a step on each beat. On the last beat she finishes facing the audience in a high 2nd position. The turning phrase has been interrupted. Her head is tilted left and rotated right. Did she hear something?

[5] With a slight accent at the start, she raises her arms, her relaxed hands being placed behind her ears, palms facing forward as if listening. Her gaze is downward towards the left. It was nothing. He is not there. She lowers her arms while lowering her heels, 'rocking' first to the right and then to the left. On the last beat she repeats the fast turn from the end of [3] but ends facing downstage left in a lunge on the right foot similar to the first lunge in [1]. During the first two beats her rounded left arm reaches forward to the downstage left corner, her left shoulder area being included as the arm rotates inward. Her focus is downward and to the right. She holds.[12] Her torso comes upright and then leans into the back left diagonal, her arms opening to the side and rotating outwards. Her focus is diagonally backwards into the direction in which she leans.[13] Now, on count 6, she breaks the mood and with a quick high step backwards on the left foot, her right leg lifts high forward as her body arches backwards with a forward high focus.

[7] Starting with a *tombé*, she swiftly runs forward toward downstage left. She then performs an *assemblé* traveling into the same direction in which she was running, at the same time turning a quarter to the right ending in a parallel 1st position, chest tilted away to her right, arms out to the side while her focus is still lifted high towards the downstage left corner of the stage. A briefer run follows again to the downstage left, followed by a similar *assemblé* turning to the left. At the last moment on count 6, she quickly pivots to the left rising on both feet, her arms flung high to the side. Focusing back to where she commenced the solo, she

---

[12] Note the importance of the pauses which help to establish the rhythm of the phrase.

[13] These six measures have given the impression of being alone, enjoying her own beauty while still being aware that her lover is nearby. It is a small study in introversion.

runs swiftly along the stage diagonal to the upstage right corner. This run ends in a bigger *assemblé* which is similar to the two just performed. While in the air she turns to the left and ends facing the audience.[14]

[9-10] In contrast to the previous traveling she now dances rapturously on the spot. Rising on her right foot, she steps at the same time across with her left into a full *soutenu* (swivel) turn to the right. During the turn her chest inclines to the left and rolls around to the right. Her rounded arms are held out to the side. The turn ends facing the audience with a spring into parallel 1st position, chest tilted left, the focus forward high. The turning now continues, two complete turns being made during six small springs while the focus remains up. The last spring ends in a deeper *plié* from which she rises on her left leg, right knee crossed high above the other knee, her right hand taking her right knee, her left hand placed on her right, and her chest twisted in opposition thus causing a tautness that both stabilizes the balance and gives a finality to the phrase. She holds two counts.

[11-12] With a swift *soutenu* turn to the left in one count, body and arms similar to the first turn in [9], she does a small *assemblé* landing in 1st position as a preparation for a repeat of the series of small springs in 1st which continue counterclockwise until the end of [12]. This time to heighten the rhapsody of the turns her head rolls in any direction while she turns many times to the left. Her arms, still out to the side, may change height, and be rounded one arm after the other. Except for the basic structure, and especially the rhythm, the dancer builds her own phrase in use of arms, focus, chest and head.

[13-14] The turning climaxes on a loud chord in the music as the dancer, facing downstage left, drops into a very deep *plié* on the right foot, left extended forward with toe touching the floor. Her body is rounded forward parallel to the floor, arms are down over the foot, rounded and rotated inward. Hold. From this stillness she slowly begins to raise her left leg to a long front *attitude*, arms rising forward with the leg, the torso, however, staying down as long as possible. With a lessening of the *plié* the leg now slowly circles around to the highest possible *attitude*. The arms accompany the circle of the leg and end back towards the diagonals, the chest is arched backward, the focus is forward high.

[15-17] With a deepening of the *plié* she prepares for a rise before the *tombé* which initiates the fastest of runs down the length of the diagonal to downstage left. A quick high forward step and turn reverses direction and she suspends in a high 4th, her chest arched backwards, arms stretched high to the side. After a brief pause she *tombés* again into a run along the diagonal ending with a traveling *assemblé* turning to the right landing in a parallel 1st facing upstage for the first time. During this entire sequence of runs on the diagonal the intensity and expectation have been building. Now she pauses as her lover enters from the corner and, with a similar *assemblé* ending facing upstage, he arrives at her left side so that their high inside arms touch as they lean away from one another.

---

[14] These eight measures show a use of space that the choreographer often employs. She restricts herself to one line of direction and choreographs extended phrases to satisfy this restriction. This is not a mechanical device but a motivated one. The focus for the entire eight measures is along the stage diagonal from where she first entered to where her lover may have exited.

[18]   After a dramatic stillness the man places his arm around her waist looking at her. As their outside arms lower, she reciprocates. The stillness both before and after the 'embracing' emphasises the reunion. She lets go his waist and lowers her arm as she quickly changes side, turning as she passes in front of him. Their other arms now 'embrace' their partner's waist.

[19-20]   Slowly they breath in, rising to a suspension, chest arched backward, outside arms rising high and the focus still on one another.   Lowering their arms, they gently *tombé* backwards into a short easy backward run.   This run gradually slows down into a walk becoming progressively slower.   Walking in unison, they both end stepping backwards on the right, leaving the left foot touching in front.   The backward arch in the chest slowly disappears but they remain looking at one another.[15]

The couple is now downstage right. As they pause the other couple enters from upstage left. P is downstage of H and they are holding hands. Their entrance must capture the mood of the other couple. Thus the end of one dance becomes the beginning of the next.

Poem: Two Duets

[1-6]   Each couple now takes a walk on their own. The music although written in 9/8 is heard as 3/4. With their inside arms around each other's waist, and facing upstage, the downstage right dancers (K and W) now retrace their path upstage stepping on irregular counts.

At the same time the second couple (P and H) has a more complex phrase.   The woman gestures forward low sharply to take a long step onto the right foot, the left leg lifting quickly into *arabesque* parallel to the floor. At the same time her torso tilts forward turning enough so that she may look back at her partner who performs the same step pattern in syncopation one count later.   These first two steps establish a syncopation which continues throughout the walk. They now continue with a *developpé* to the front which passes through a high *retiré*. As the leg extends forward the torso inclines backward, again to facilitate looking at one another. The woman may have to turn her leg in **slightly** on the *passé* to bring it through.

The man repeats this pattern to the other side ending with an additional step on the right into *arabesque*. The woman performs the pattern three times taking an additional step on the left [4]. While the man holds, she rises looking upward, her right arm opening to the side. As she rises he lowers to a large 4th position lunge, left foot back. She now lowers through a *tombé* step to her left, and ends by taking her left foot back into a similar 4th position lunge. She moulds herself to the front of his upright torso. As their arms come down to their sides and their hands touch (the man being on the inside), she rests her cheek on his chest. Simultaneous with the final step by the other couple [5], P rises to half-toe as he feels her cheek on him. His arms float out to the side and he slowly lowers to the lunge position in which he started.

---

[15] Another movement characteristic of Sokolow's work is the high uplifted arch of the chest. She has said that she was very inspired by the Isadora Duncan dancing that she saw performed by the Duncan disciples. To achieve this high open arch, the front of the chest must relax so that the chest may lie backwards with a feeling of openness to it. In many of her works the chest arches so far back (with the head even more back) that from the audience the head disappears, creating a beautiful line across the shoulders.

A pause follows. W, the woman in the first couple, now leaves her man K by doing a slow rise in 1st position as she pivots to the left as preparation for a smooth run in a small circle passing behind him before exiting upstage right. Realizing that she has gone he also rises turning to face the audience and then lowering, but it is too late to see her exiting to his left. He holds until [7] count 3, and then after another rise and lowering commences a broken run ending with a high step into 4th. Still looking for her he leaves the stage by running around clockwise exiting at the upstage left corner, passing behind the other couple.

[7-8] The other couple have continued their love duet during this parting. H, the woman, reaches out far to the right and forward as she 'embraces' him ending with her right hand on his left shoulder. The touch of her hand motivates him to do likewise with his left arm, his hand ending touching her right upper arm. This causes her left arm to reach out and encircle them both thus ending with her left hand on her own right upper arm. They are now completely wrapped in one another's arms. Now their heads circle in different directions and with different timing. Each is reacting to the embrace. The first motion for the roll is forward with a downward heaviness.

[9-10] As her head concludes its roll, H's left arm reaches forward and around to the left to end wrapped around his back. (The other couple has now left the stage.) P's left arm now does the same circling forward, ending in a final embrace.[16]

[11-13] They break away from one another, almost pushing themselves apart. He takes a large step backwards arms flung to the side, chest arched back, while a second later she takes a large step forward rising into a 4th position, arms flung wide with the chest and head flung back. They now run short broken phrases with abrupt pauses in a high 4th or 1st position. All directional changes are fast and motivated by their separation.

[13-14] When he arrives in the upstage left corner, he turns to the downstage diagonal and sees her. She runs upstage on this diagonal stopping immediately in front of him. "Will you forgive me?" she seems to ask as she lowers her head. He reaches out to her with his right hand. She takes it, a pause, and he swiftly pulls her in to his left side. She makes a half-turn as she comes in, his left arm ending around her waist and her left hand taking his left hand at her side. They look at one another as they rise in preparation for the next phrase.

[15-21] In contrast to all that has gone before in the two duets the dancers now quickly cross and recross the stage with a simple traveling phrase of step-hop in low *arabesque* with the torso upright, followed by a *cabriole* forward for which the torso leans backwards. At the start the rhythm of the footwork is clearly heard in the music, now written in 3/4, but as the music progresses the tempo of the music slows down. The dancers, however, **must** keep the same dance pulse in contrast to the ritardando of the music pulse. This type of step pattern is more usually performed in a ternary rhythm; here though, the dancers must give more attack to the movement and hence use a binary rhythm, i.e. in two. It is quite a challenge for the dancers not to slip into a three or slow down the tempo of the movement. This traveling section

---

[16] This moment is another Sokolow characteristic. The embracing and passion have become too much. There is only one thing left to do - break free.

commences with couple H and P moving on the diagonal to downstage right. Next comes K from downstage left and W from upstage right, both crossing on the diagonal. The dancers continue to enter dancing on the diagonals which are the longest straight path that a dancer can traverse on stage. There should be an on-goingness to the phrase as the dancers, united, enjoy dancing together. P and H end on stage with a step on their left foot followed by a moment of stillness. At no time during these crossings is the stage ever empty.

[22-27] Slowly the choreographic statement breaks up as the other dancers run in, pause and regroup. P pulls away from H traveling parallel to the front of the stage. H runs forward and exits downstage right [27]. W re-enters from upstage right and runs a circular path to end center stage. Immediately following W's entrance, K enters from downstage left and crosses to center stage, passing downstage of P. K finds W upstage center and, joining her, places his left arm around her waist. A moment of stillness follows.

[24-29] On [24] the music changes back to 9/8, the metre of the first two duets. Again the dancers count a three but these counts do not agree with the music measures. The dancers start one count ahead, i.e., '(1)' equals (7,8,9) in the music. W steps forward on his left foot and quickly raises his right leg forward to hip height. As he rounds his body forward parallel to the floor K (the woman) picks up the movement starting on the left foot. He then *pliés*, his foot touching the floor in front while she lowers her torso and touches the floor with her foot. Both now lower their torsos further in unison until the head is near the foot. In unison both dancers roll their heads to the left a full circle ending tilted to the left. The movement is large and includes the chest somewhat. The walking phrase is now repeated to the opposite side and ends with only a half-circular roll of the head to the right, the head ending inclined to the left. P, who has been watching W and K, decides just before [26] to run off. He passes around W and K before exiting downstage right.

[28-29] In a large circular movement W now lowers her right arm and moves it across the front of her body with an accompanying chest tilt to the left. Sweeping her arm down she opens it out to the right to end embracing K's chest from behind. At the same time she inclines her chest towards him. K, meanwhile, indicates with a gesture of his right arm toward the downstage area of the stage where he wishes them both to travel next.

[30-31] Gazing at one another, with K leading the way, they begin a syncopated walk each step being into an *arabesque*, the torso forward. This syncopation can be heard in the music. At the same time P and H enter from the upstage right corner. They are holding hands the woman being downstage of the man. They walk at a slower tempo than the other couple, taking a step first on the right foot and then holding for the duration of two steps performed by the other couple. They take three steps in all, one in each measure, ending on the right foot.

[32-34] Couple W and K now slowly swing their free leg forward and backwards, hip height and in opposition, K starting forward first. K performs three swings, W only two. W closes in a high 5th position raising her left arm to the side. She then walks away from K, turning to face him and offers her arms to him as she steps into a 'backward' lunge, the back leg being bent, the foot on the forced arch. He rises in 1st before she has completed her rise in 5th and turns to stage right to face her while lowering his weight into a similar 4th position 'backward' lunge as he reaches for her. They are now facing one another, parallel to the audience with

torsos contracted forward, their focus being down to the floor. Meanwhile, [33] the other couple have ceased traveling and, while holding the left leg in a low *retiré*, lower the rounded torso forward until the head is near the floor. They then rise to the highest *attitude* with the torso forward high and spiralling to the left. Their arms rise to the side completing the line. Their focus is out to the front of the stage.

[34] As P and H take this *attitude* the other couple begins to separate. W rises onto her left foot to a high *arabesque*, torso lifted, the chest continuing to arch slowly backwards. (They are still holding hands.)

[35-36] With the quickest of *fouettés* W turns away from K, throwing her arms high out to the side, and, still arched, suspends before commencing a broken running phrase. As she begins to run, K steps back, coming upright, his 'empty' arms extended to where she was. He now commences to run, searching for her. [35] P breaks from his partner by stepping forward into a rising turn to the right ending with his right leg to the side, his right arm lifted above his head and his left arm to the side. He now begins his broken running phrase. H holds until, with the same turning step, she starts to run, leaving to search for him.

[37-39] All the dancers are now in different areas of the stage, facing different directions (but not facing one another). In unison they slowly rise with an inward breath, the right leg raised to a high *arabesque*, arms rotated outward and opened sideward. One by one they run off. H and K to stage right, P to upstage left. W remains downstage left. She is alone. Beginning with two turning *chassé coupés*, she runs to upstage right exiting with a climactic *grand jeté*.

[40-47] All dancers now enter and re-enter crossing the stage with either step-hop-*cabriole* or a run ending with a *grand jeté*. The last to enter in [47] is P who comes from upstage left with the step-hop-*cabriole* combination traveling on the diagonal. He comes to a halt. The dancing stops. He realizes that everybody else has gone. Where is his lover? He now begins a broken running phrase back on the same diagonal, a run that gradually fades out. Ending almost center stage, in a casual 1st position, facing downstage right, arms by his side he gazes out into the distance.

By now the reader of *Ballade* may have noticed how often the dancers are told to run in any direction, face any direction and do any of a set of phrases that have already been performed. This way of working shows great trust between choreographer and dancers. When told to run anywhere for example, the choreographer is not giving the dancer complete freedom. The choices must be made within the structure of the choreography and within the dramatic content of the piece. That is to say, if the dancers are searching for a lover they will not run towards them, but into an area of the stage far removed from them. If they are in an angry mood they will not run long curved and sweeping paths but short, broken and straight paths. When told to end facing in any direction they will seldom face one another especially if there is to be a feeling of distance and non-communication between them. This way of working gives the dancer a feeling of being involved in the creative process, but more than this it shows that the choreographer knows that her dancers understand how she works. Therefore when reading or reconstructing this dance first find the motivation and then a solution.

Man's Solo

As described in the introduction, this solo was inspired by images of Nijinsky. The dancer should bring this inspiration to the solo, not a classical ballet approach, but the sensuous and animalistic quality of movement that has been described as Nijinsky's.

[1-8] The dancer springs to the left sinking into a deep *plié* while brushing his right leg in a circular pattern, across to the left forward diagonal. His hands are grasped behind his back. As he lands his torso is stretched on the right side and curved over to the left. At the same time that his torso is twisting to the left, his head is rotating in opposition to the right. He repeats this step, springing to the right and again to the left. He then flings his right arm out high to the side. Slowly raising his whole arm up and turning it inwards, he bends it, bringing the hand down to touch his left ear. On count 8 his head comes vertical and his focus is directed to the right high diagonal.

[9-16] Maintaining his hand pressing against his ear he repeats the springing phrase to the right and to the left. He holds for a brief pause while his head and focus return to normal. He arches his torso further to the left, and then rolls forward and downward until his head is almost at floor level. He then sequentially rolls through the torso until he is leaning backward high, arms opening out to the side, his foot touching the floor in front. The dancer is now in the longest possible line from toe to head. Still leaning backward he runs backwards on the diagonal to the upstage left corner of the stage, ending on his left foot, right foot extended in front with the toe touching the floor (the same position in which he started the run). At the end of [16] he faces the audience. He 'winds' up to the left by tilting and turning his chest to the left while his right arm crosses in front.

[17-23] He now takes a deep sideward *chassé coupé* turn as preparation for a turning leap to the right leaning diagonally backward into the direction of the turn. His rounded right arm lifts high to help him at the highest point of the leap. This slow preparation leads into the same pattern performed swiftly three times across the back of the stage. The last one ends with a step to the right in *plié* to face downstage left followed by a long step back onto the left concluding in a rise in 1st position. As his arms rise to the side his chest arches backwards.

[24-32] A moment of suspension leads into a swift run halfway down the diagonal, his arms pulled back, his focus far forward. He drops down into the same forward low torso position as in [12] and then, torso upright, quickly does a half *soutenu* turn to the right with a *renversé* in the torso, i.e. allowing his chest to roll around to the left, backwards and to the right while the arms are again pulled backwards. He repeats the run, the drop and the turn ending upstage where he first started this pattern.

[33-52] Another swift run ends in a high 4th position, his left foot forward, left arm to the side and right arm rounded in front. A buoyant uplift for two measures is followed by his right arm swinging around to the right and ending above his head. The arm movement facilitates the full turn to the right on the left foot (the right leg extended low in front). This turn ends in a high 4th position, the right foot forward. His right arm now completes a low lasso-like movement over his head ending with the arm circling forward and opening out to the

side. As his arm opens to the side his chest twists to the right. This twist in the chest quickly disappears as he runs a shorter path, still on the same diagonal. He ends in a high 4th position with his right foot forward and his right arm forward and rounded. He repeats the turn and lasso arm movement. This time the lasso movement and chest twist lead into a turn to the right to face stage right as a preparation for a *chassé* upstage followed by fast *enchaîné* turns traveling upstage. He ends facing upstage in a high 1st position. His focus is forward high, there is a slight spiral in the body and his hands end near his ears (as if he hears something); he then turns right to face downstage.

[53-69] The sideward springing pattern is now repeated four times moving first to the left. Then with arms thrown outward, chest arched and his head back so far that it cannot be seen by the audience, he takes a step into a large *assemblé* traveling to the right. The landing rebounds into a high 1st position. He holds one measure. Now follow four consecutive slow *assemblés*, the chest and head positions being maintained while he travels across the stage from left to right. The opening phrase is repeated four times, this time circling one full circle to the right. He springs out of this to a high 5th position facing the audience, hands still grasped behind his back. Now his shoulders are drawn forward and in as he looks downward at his own reflection in the water.

[70-114] Admiring his reflection he now begins sequentially to twist his chest to the right and left, gradually allowing his shoulders to circle as the movement grows in intensity. The successions begin to overlap and his right arm rises to the side. At the peak of this phrase he swiftly brings his right arm down behind his back, arches back over his left shoulder. This arch includes the head thus giving prominence to the stretch of the right side of the neck. He then pivots on the right foot into a full turn to end in a 4th position, left foot forward. Stillness follows, the high arched position is held. The turn and the arched position are then reversed and again followed by stillness. This turn and pause are again repeated. He now bursts free and, as the choreographer said, *"Falls in love with the music"*. He runs like the wind in a large counterclockwise circle around the stage performing a free combination of leaps, runs and *chassé* turns. After one and a half circles he comes to center stage and ends in a high 1st position, arms flung out to the side. The briefest of pauses is followed by a high spring into the air in which his body arches over the left. As he lands he moves sequentially down into a side fall to the right. This is followed by a quick recovery to a sitting position, his torso leaning to the right, head upright, weight taken by his right hand placed out to the side. His right leg is fully extended to the left and his left leg is tightly drawn in. His left arm rests on top of his left knee. Hold [108]. Now his head rolls freely several times to the left. As this head roll ends, his torso whips into a tight, rounded shape, spiralling to the left, his right leg is drawn in and his right arm crosses the body and 'grasps the entire shape'. His head is also very low helping to create this smallest and tightest of positions. Holding for one measure [113], he then quickly unwinds to the vertical with a spiral to the right. His right arm swings around to the right and ends with his hand touching the back of his head. The picture is completed with a focus that is forward and upward.

Ending

The end typifies some of the earlier comments on the style of this work. The lovers are quarrelling, therefore the rhythms will be unpredictable, and the intention is more important than the resulting shapes.

[1-5] P holds the final position from his solo. The other dancers burst onto the stage with the highest possible energy, first W [3] and then H [4] and K in [5]. W performs what is to be the theme for this section. A fast, high energy run is abruptly halted when the dancer 'throws' herself into a deep *plié* on the left foot, right toe touching the floor in front, the chest rounding inwards, the torso low forward, the head almost touching the floor. At the same time the arms are thrust downwards, the left hand grasping the right wrist. This position is held. Then with a feeling of abandonment, as if tearing herself apart, the dancer suddenly rises with a half-turn to the right on the highest of forced arches and, at the same time, stretches her arms, well rotated outward, to the side. At the same moment her right leg also opens outward to a high sideward position. Her torso stretches upward as high as possible, the chest arching backwards so that the head 'disappears'. (The movement feels as if you have turned yourself inside out.) She holds. Again she runs as if pushed to repeat the theme. The variations on the theme may be performed on either leg, rising to face any direction and running into any direction, even a direction other than that faced at the end of a rise. The dancer may turn on the rise or not turn. The holds maybe a brief 1/8 note (quaver), or much longer, an entire measure. These decisions depend on when other dancers are moving. The unpredictable pulse is achieved with the quick drop into *plié*. No two dancers should be doing this drop at the same time.

[3-12] The above thematic material is used by all dancers up to [12].

[11-15] The music has now accelerated and P rises as fast as possible to a high arch in 5th, right foot in front, arms down by the side. He again looks downward but slowly raises his head to end looking at H. By this time each dancer has stopped in front of his/her partner. In the silence of [12], P lunges far forward on his left foot, his right arm reaching forward to H, his torso leaning forward. He commands her to come to him. She responds with a lunge on the right, extending both arms forward to grasp his extended right hand. Abruptly he pulls her to himself and as she turns she becomes wrapped in his arm. He ends facing downstage, she ends pressed against him facing upstage. As if to show his possessiveness he tightly embraces her with his right arm. The other couple do likewise, K lunging on [13] and W on [14]. Again it is the thrust and high energy of the lunge which gives the continued dramatic rhythm. There is no musical rhythm to this section of the dance; except for an occasional music cue the dancers are cueing from each other.

[15-20] Immediately after the embrace the men separate from the women with a short and fast *chaîné*. They again end in a lunge but there is no need to extend the arm. The women know and respond by hurling themselves at the feet of the men, their torsos arched backwards parallel to the floor. [17] H turns on right knee to face P. Her torso holds its position in space to end rounded forward. With a large *rond de jambe* of his right leg P steps over H. He ends in a deep lunge and his hands take hers. K simply steps in to his partner, lunges over her and takes her hands. Slowly on [19-20] (an ascending music cue), they raise the women to standing in

4th on the forced arch. Arms and focus are both up to the sky. Stillness follows.

[22-26] The silence is broken by their arms being brought down to their sides in uneven timing. Moving a beat apart, the women swiftly turn to face their partners and drop into a 4th position *plié*, chest arched backwards and hands clasped behind the man's neck. They appear as if they are hanging there. Still one beat apart they look downward. Now, as if to right everything, the women adjust themselves to stand by the left side of their partner. Everybody is facing the audience, the man clasps the woman's hand and they look at one another.

[27-39] They now commence a brief running phrase. K and W start first running backwards, their hands release and W travels a little further than K ending in a high 1st position, focus forward and upward. As soon as they have commenced their run, the other couple start running forward, their hands also release and P travels a little further ending as the other couple ended. The couples now break and run to different areas of the stage. Each in turn will commence the earlier theme or variation on the theme. This time K and P drop together followed by W and then H. This theme is repeated several times. These two measures act as a transition for the dancers to come together (though still some distance apart).

[40-45] As a preparation for the highest spring they can achieve, all four lovers now step forward into a *plié*, body folded forward and arms crossed in front of the torso. They hurl themselves into the air into the highest possible *sauté* in *attitude*, chest arched as far back as possible and arms thrown upward to the wind. In the tradition of 'good old modern dance' they fall to the floor rolling out through the torso, arms splayed out behind them. They recover quickly by coming to a sitting position led by the chest and then rise to standing. In such a jump Sokolow expects to see the energy needed to hurl yourself into the air. The line may be balletic but the performance is not. All dancers are now facing a new direction into which they run. Again they hurl themselves into the air and again recover to a sitting position. P and H arrive upstage center, W and K end downstage left.

[46-55] The men reach forward first with one arm then with the other arm. Their women respond by quickly taking their hands. On another ascending music cue [52-53] they rise to standing. The climax has been reached. The men reach and tightly embrace their women. The embrace is smothering. The women cannot stand the closeness of the men and violently push themselves free. The push occurs on the first of the repeated chords in the music. All dancers then separate further by jumping from two feet to two feet as they spread about the stage. The jumps are now in an even rhythm. After a few jumps which will continually change direction, the dancers slowly straighten up from the *plié*. As they 'rise' their arms reach out as if to talk to their partner or to speak to empty space, or to address the audience. The phrase is repeated as many times as needed while the curtain comes in.

It is this type of ending, one of despair and loneliness after an uplifting and poetically beautiful dance, that has caused some critics to call the choreographer the mistress of gloom and doom. But as Anna Sokolow said in rehearsal, "This is life".

As strange as this statement may seem, it is 'a moment of lyricism' - not the soft and flowing representational lyricism to which dance audiences are accustomed, but a more imaginative one in tune with the twentieth century.

"True lyricism has to have passion and steel beneath it. For an arm to come up beautifully and with meaning it has to have great power and energy". This recollection by Jeff Duncan from an audition by Anna Sokolow is a key to her lyricism and the kinaesthetic and emotional response an audience feels from her choreography.   There is an emotional pull to the choreography which is felt from the first rapturous run across the stage as the dancers seek their lovers, through the expansive sections and into the personal moments which culminate in the final moments of search and rejection.

Throughout this dance the movement is clear and simple yet it is always emotionally charged. It would be quite wrong to look at the simplicity of the score and deduce that this is an easy dance to perform. It isn't. The expressive range is quite wide and requires intensive coaching on the part of the director. The dancers should be coached as actors are. They should be fed stimulating images that bring forth the restlessness and inconclusiveness of young lovers.

Another overlooked aspect of *Ballade* is that it is void of sets, props or any trimmings, including movement, to suggest a period. It has been suggested that Jerome Robbins' *Dancers at a Gathering* was inspired by *Ballade*. (He certainly admires Sokolow's work.)   After the simple expressiveness of choreography and the music in both *Ballade* and *Dancers at a Gathering* it will be difficult for future choreographers to return to the often cumbersome handling of lyrical and romantic themes.

Ballade has not been seen very often. It is difficult to find writings on the piece. It came, as it were, like a spring shower upon the dance scene of the early sixties and lasted just long enough to make an impact on twentieth century choreography; to spawn a style that has remained until today and should be here for generations to come. If it were not for the dance score Sokolow's contribution to this genre of dance could be lost forever.

LABANOTATION GLOSSARY

Turnout key throughout, except for steps such as *cabrioles,* and *enchaîné* turns.

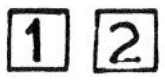

Dancers' counts (Opening, meas. 13)

Measure numbers repeated on recto page (Opening, meas. 28)

With uplift (Opening Continued, meas. 29)

Sustained uplift during the springs (Quartet, meas. 11)

With weight (Woman's Solo, meas. 6)

Gentle, fine touch (Opening, meas. 23)

Strong (Man's Solo, meas. 79)

Relaxed (Man's Solo, meas. 107)

Emphasized (Opening, meas. 22)

Unemphasized (Opening, meas. 26)

Float (Man's Solo, meas. 38)

Glide (Quartet, meas. 2)

Bound flow (Ending, meas. 5)

Light (Quartet, meas. 4)

Light accent (Opening, meas. 18)

Strong accent (Poem: Two Duets, meas. 11)

Stronger accent (Ending, meas. 5)

Strongest accent, as strong as possible (Ending, meas. 5)

Increase in speed (Poem: Two Duets, meas. 13)

Decrease in speed (Woman's Solo, meas. 20)

Movement decelerates, like an impulse (Woman's Solo, meas. 1)

Movement occurs at approximately this moment. (Opening, meas. 27) (For exit, Opening Continued, meas. 14)

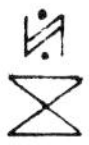

As fast as possible (Opening Continued, meas. 4)

Ad lib. duration (Quartet, meas. 13)

Part leading bow (Opening, meas. 22)

Retain effect of part leading (Woman's Solo, meas. 3)

Arm bends to achieve the end result (e.g., pulling woman in). The final position of the arm is not important. (Opening, meas. 35)

Arm draws in as needed for hand to touch designated part (Quartet, meas. 9 [W])

Gather from left side of the body
(Quartet, meas. 8)

Gather from right side of the body
(Man's Solo, meas. 69)

Arm movement leads into following position
(Opening, meas. 38)

When the arms are in either of these positions the energy must continue out beyond the fingertips. The choreographer seldom corrected the arms for an exact level or degree of flexion or rotation. On leaps either of these arm shapes were used. Movement was always more important than position.
(Quartet, meas. 11; Opening Continued meas. 11)

Back of right leg
(Quartet, meas. 8)

Any position, middle level, feet together
(Ending, meas. 55)

In all arches of the chest and in all head rolls the neck is especially emphasised. In both examples here it is the left side of the neck that would be made to feel the stretch.
(Opening, meas. 17; Quartet, meas. 7)

This high arch is very important and typical of Sokolow's choreography. It incorporates a feeling of high chest focus which conveys the outward focus of the movement.
(Opening, meas. 3)

A widening of the front of the chest to create an outward projection.
(Man's Solo, meas. 79)

Ad lib. path, see floor plan for details of path.
(Opening Continued, meas. 1)

All runs are done with relaxed knees, in a slight *plié* and always as smoothly as possible. All traveling, particularly the circular paths, need not be as precise as notated. The intention is to travel on sweeping paths that carry the dancer from one area of the stage to another.

End in a very small group ('close ranks')
(Opening, meas. 38)

Free grouping
(Opening, floor plan 38)

Freedom in direction faced
(Opening, meas. 69)

Looking at upper corners of stage itself
(Woman's Solo, meas. 7)

Repeat more or less as W
(Opening Continued, meas. 30)

Repeat dancers' counts 1-4
(Opening, meas. 15)

The movement increases in size, grows larger.
(Man's Solo, meas. 79)

Canon. Dancer A commences on count 1 and takes three steps. Dancer B commences the three steps on count 2.
(Opening, meas. 21-25)

THE DANCE SCORE

30

Quartet, meas. 4
(This section was rechoreographed for the Juilliard Ensemble production.
This moment is different to the original.)
Dancers (L to R): Alex Schlempp, Yoav Kaddar, Cathy Minn, Michele de la Reza

(Martha Swope)

OPENING

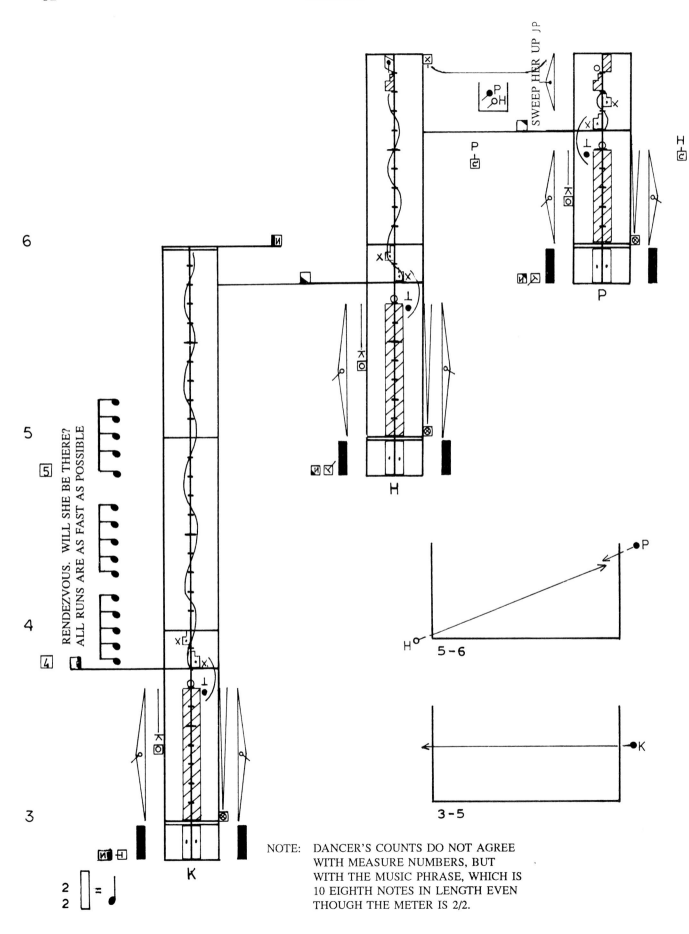

RENDEZVOUS. WILL SHE BE THERE?
ALL RUNS ARE AS FAST AS POSSIBLE

SWEEP HER UP J.P.

NOTE: DANCER'S COUNTS DO NOT AGREE
         WITH MEASURE NUMBERS, BUT
         WITH THE MUSIC PHRASE, WHICH IS
         10 EIGHTH NOTES IN LENGTH EVEN
         THOUGH THE METER IS 2/2.

W'S ENTRANCE AND EXIT TIME WILL
DEPEND ON THE SIZE OF THE STAGE. THE
STAGE SHOULD NOT BE EMPTY BEFORE P
AND H RE-ENTER. W MAY RUN THROUGH
MEASURE 12.

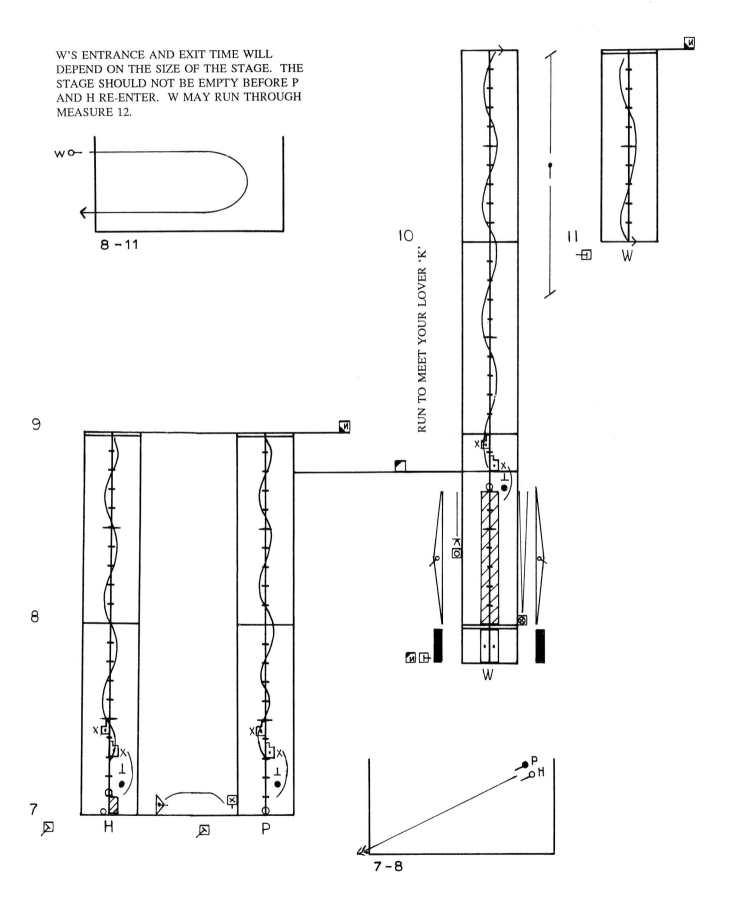

8 - 11

9

10

RUN TO MEET YOUR LOVER 'K'

11

W

8

W

7

H   P

7 - 8

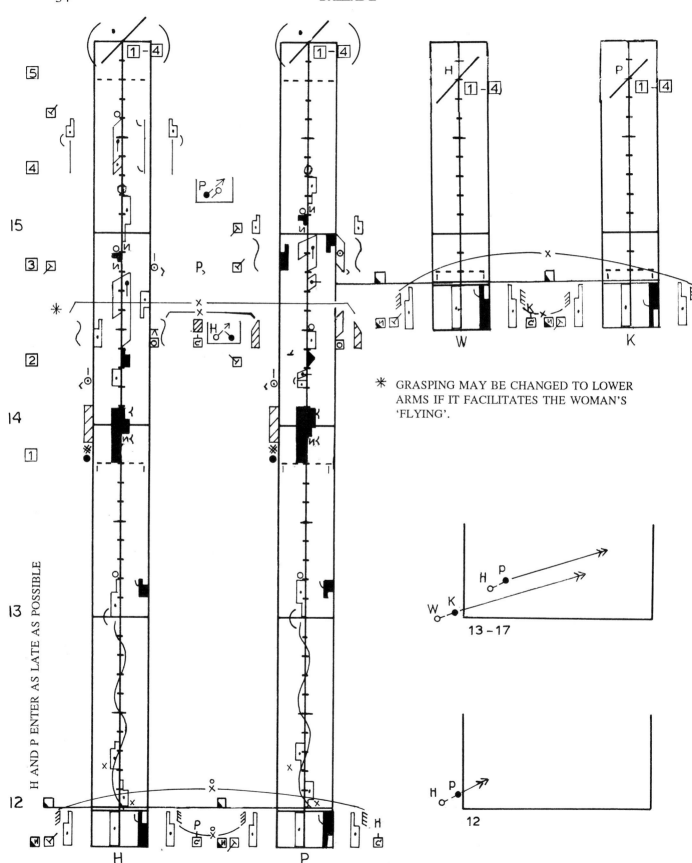

★ GRASPING MAY BE CHANGED TO LOWER
ARMS IF IT FACILITATES THE WOMAN'S
'FLYING'.

H AND P ENTER AS LATE AS POSSIBLE

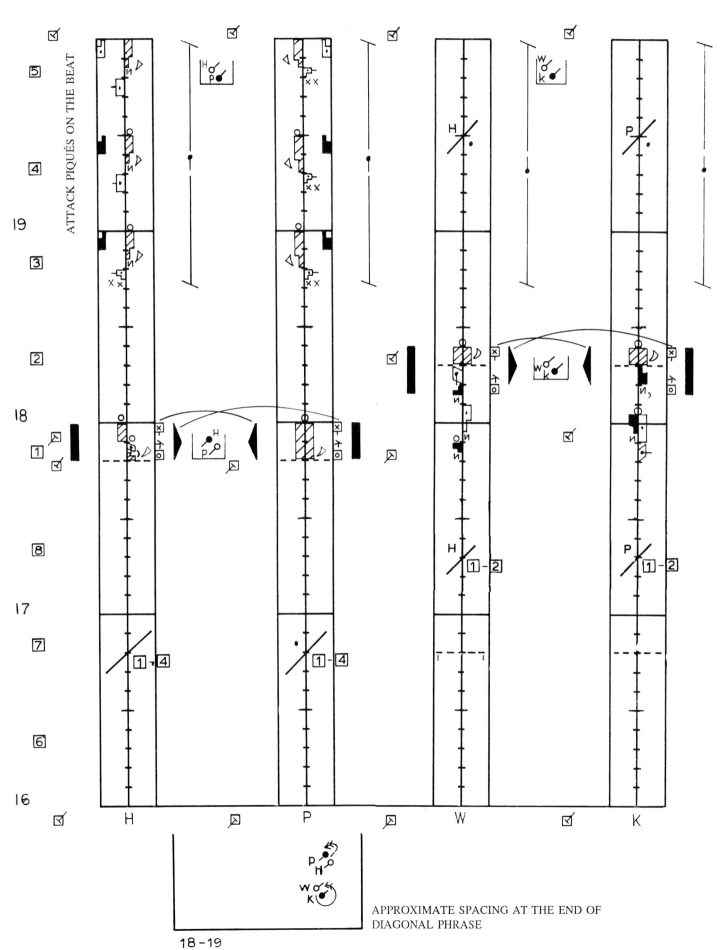

ATTACK PIQUÉS ON THE BEAT

18 – 19

APPROXIMATE SPACING AT THE END OF
DIAGONAL PHRASE

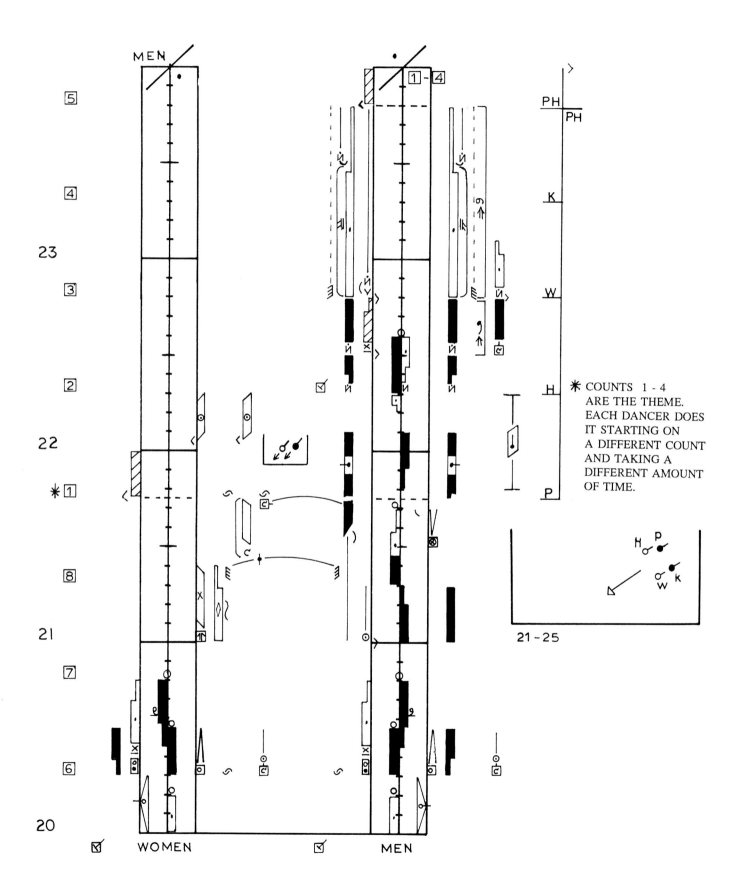

* COUNTS 1 - 4
ARE THE THEME.
EACH DANCER DOES
IT STARTING ON
A DIFFERENT COUNT
AND TAKING A
DIFFERENT AMOUNT
OF TIME.

21-25

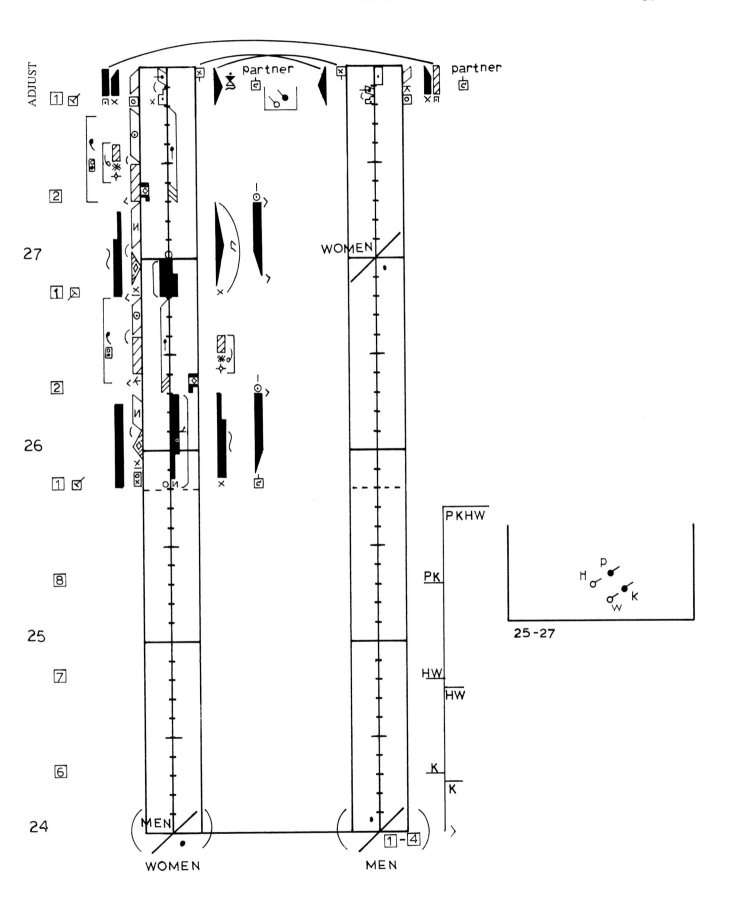

25-27

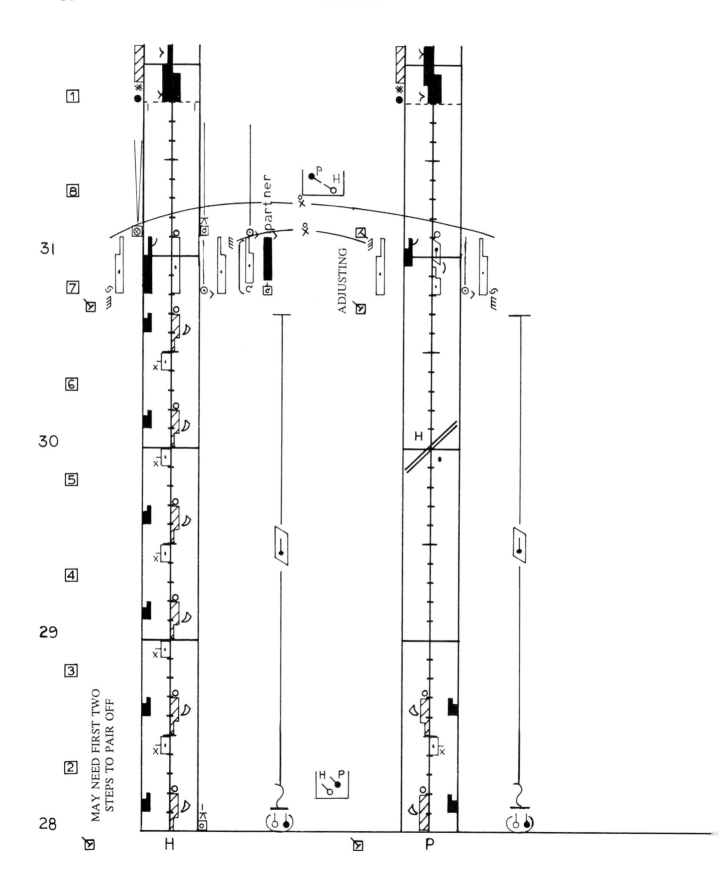

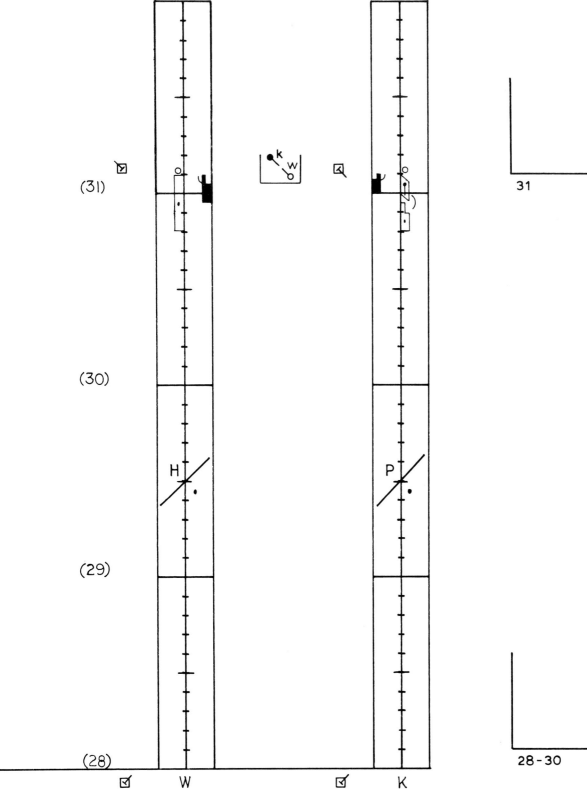

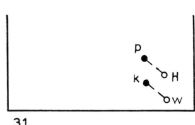

31

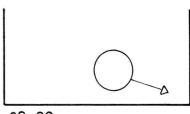

28-30

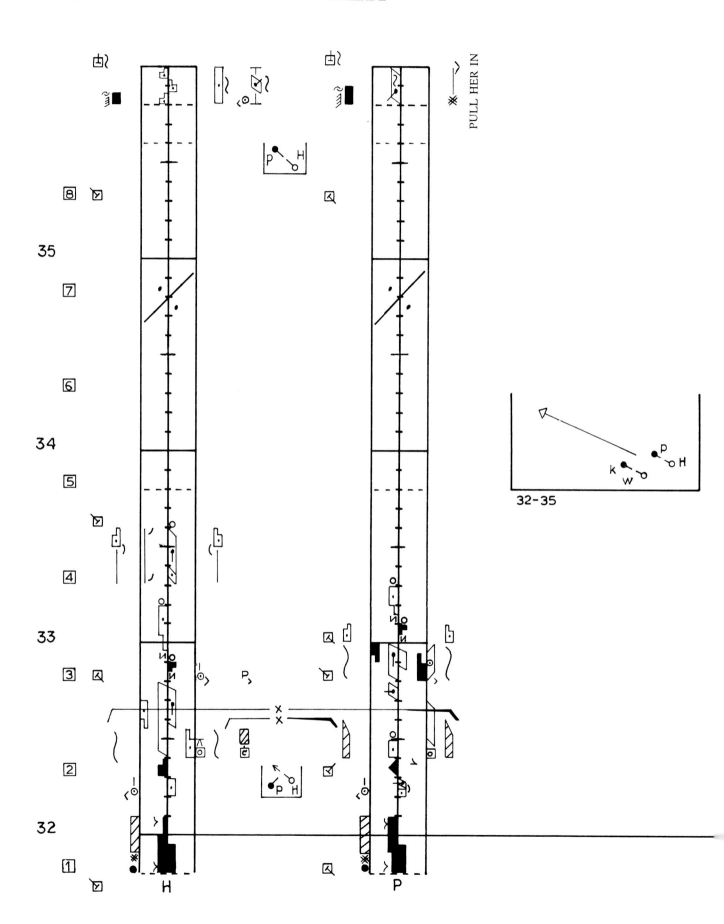

PULL HER IN

32-35

H   P

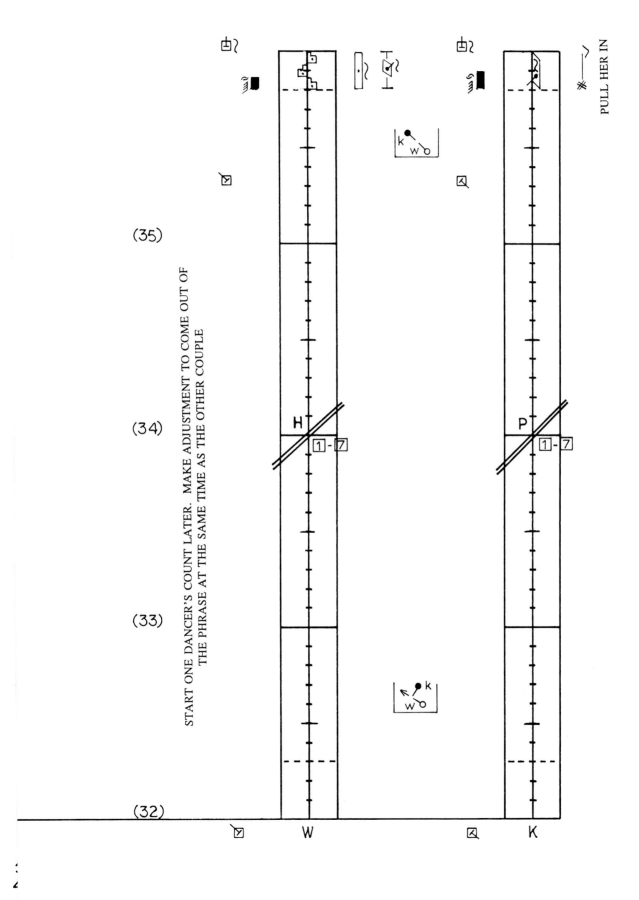

START ONE DANCER'S COUNT LATER. MAKE ADJUSTMENT TO COME OUT OF
THE PHRASE AT THE SAME TIME AS THE OTHER COUPLE

PULL HER IN

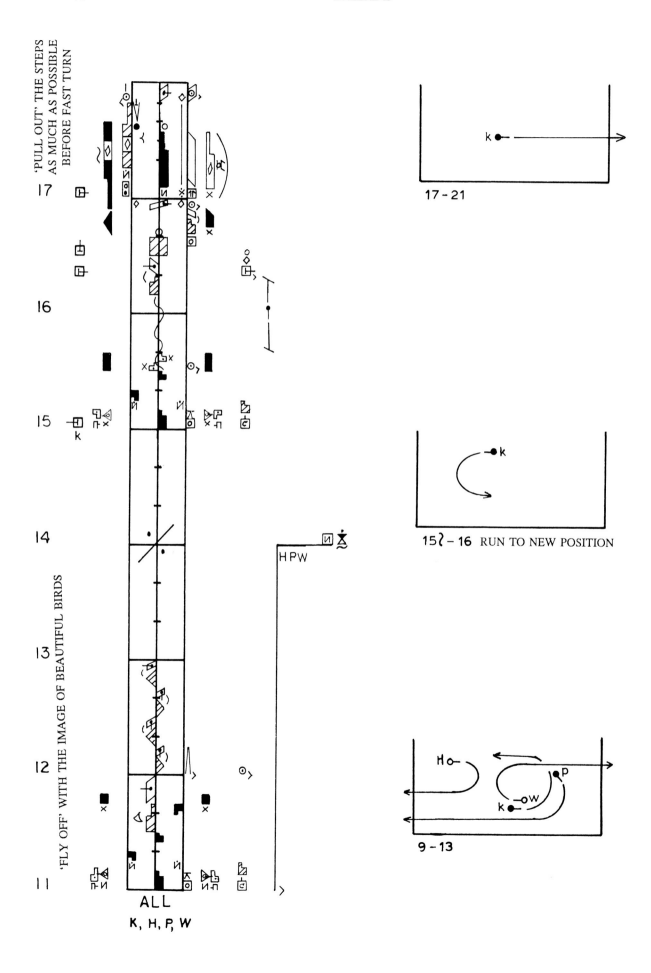

17   'PULL OUT' THE STEPS AS MUCH AS POSSIBLE BEFORE FAST TURN

16

15

14

13   'FLY OFF' WITH THE IMAGE OF BEAUTIFUL BIRDS

12

11

ALL

K, H, P, W

17 – 21

15 – 16   RUN TO NEW POSITION

9 – 13

MEAS. 22-23: EACH DANCER DOES HIS/HER
ENTRANCE PHRASE AS OFTEN AS
NECESSARY TO REACH THE SPOT WHERE
THE PATH BREAKS. AT THAT POINT, THEY
COMMENCE THE PHRASE IN MEAS. 31-32.
COVER MUCH SPACE. THE CHOREOGRAPHY
SHOULD NOT LOOK PLANNED, NOR SHOULD
IT LOOK AS IF EVERYBODY IS HEADING FOR
A CORNER.

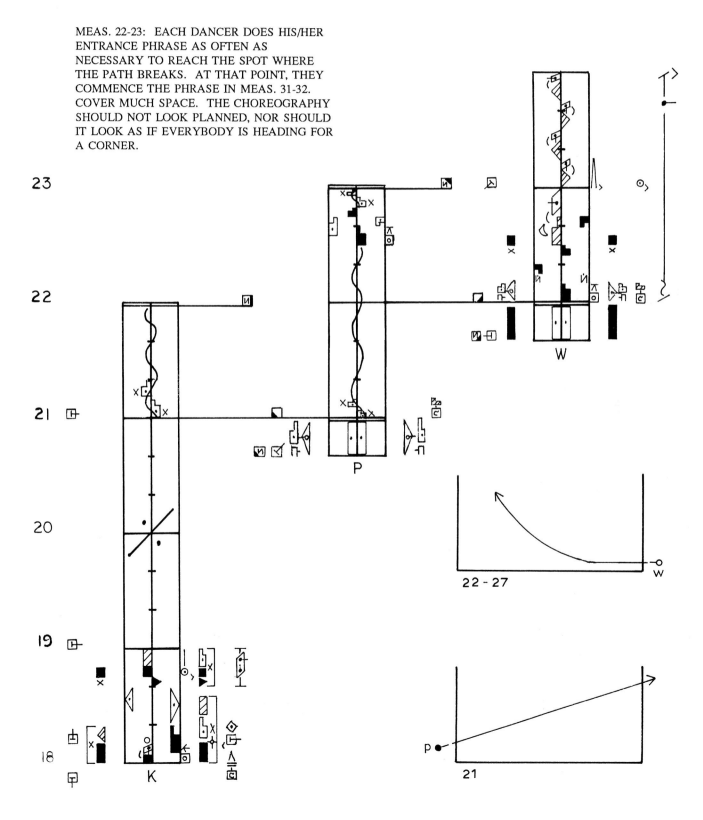

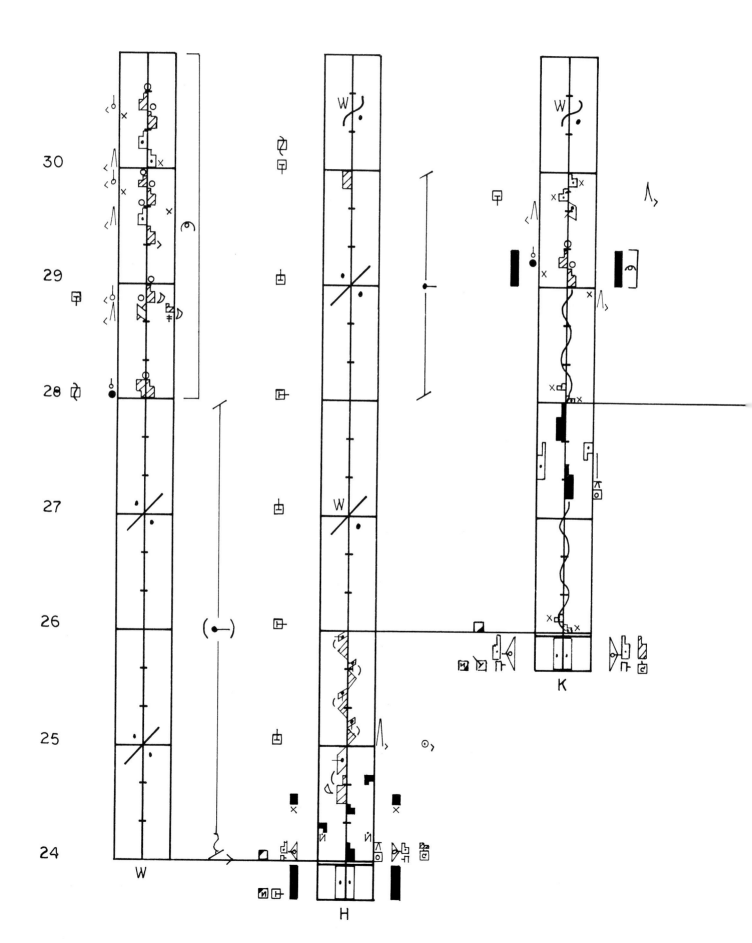

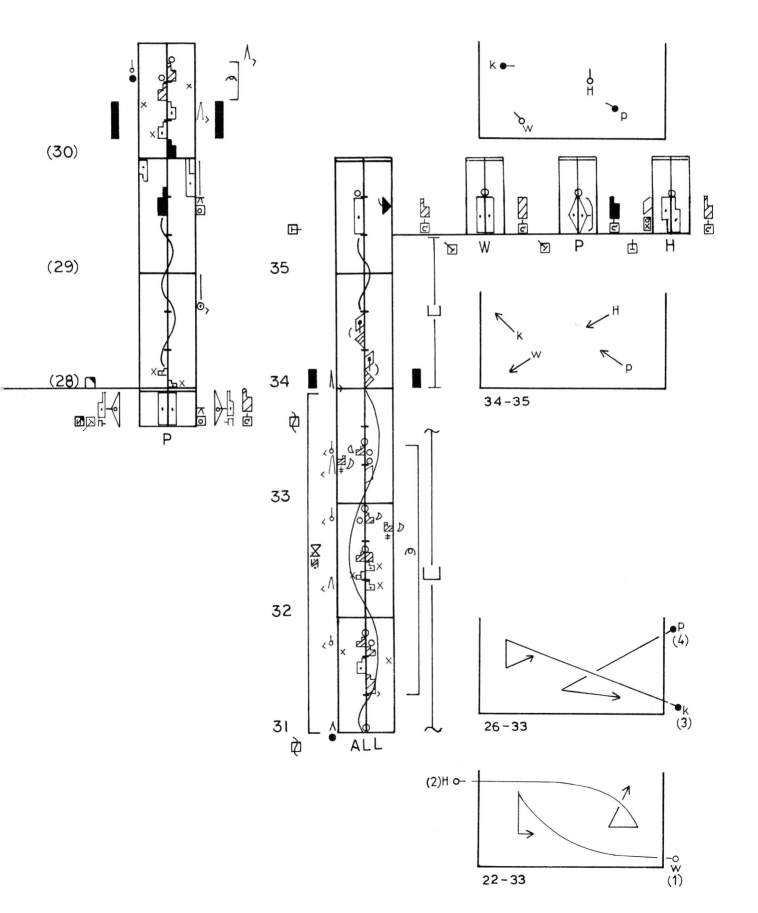

48

Quartet, meas. 4

Dancers (L to R): Eric Hampton, Dennis Nehat, Tamara Woshokiwska, Ze'eva Cohan

(Oleaga)

QUARTET

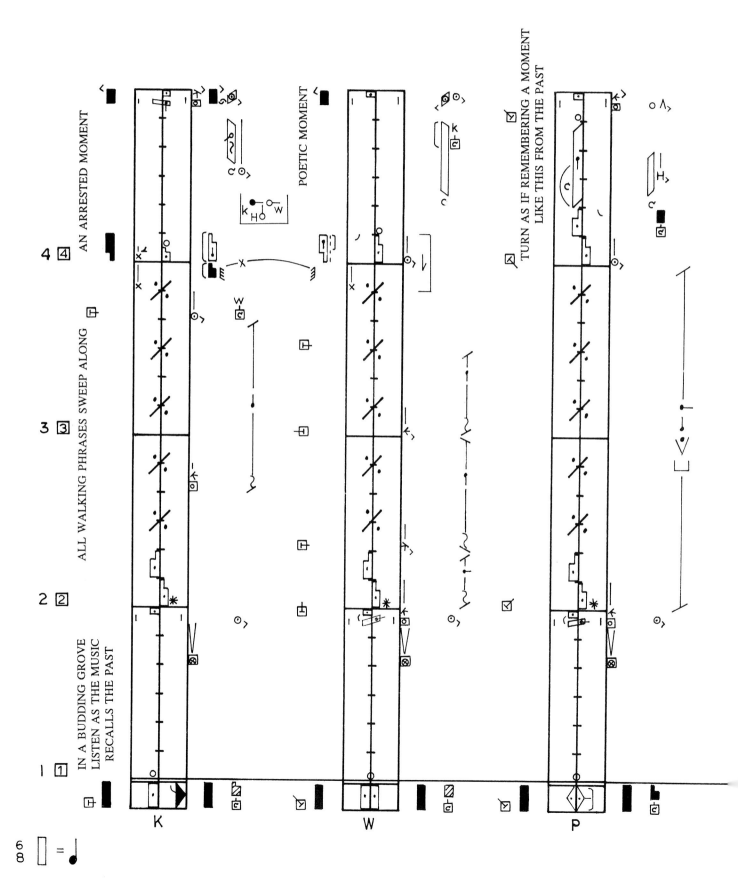

POETIC MOMENT

AN ARRESTED MOMENT

TURN AS IF REMEMBERING A MOMENT
LIKE THIS FROM THE PAST

ALL WALKING PHRASES SWEEP ALONG

IN A BUDDING GROVE
LISTEN AS THE MUSIC
RECALLS THE PAST

4 4

3 3

2 2

1 1

K

W

P

6
8 ▯ = ♪

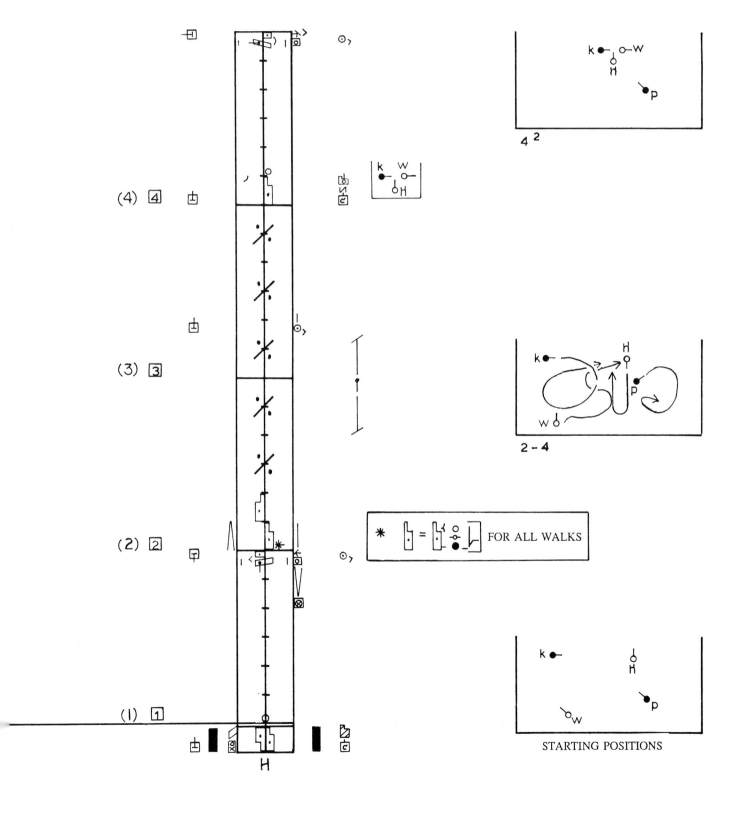

2⁴

2 - 4

* ⌐ = ⌐ FOR ALL WALKS

STARTING POSITIONS

H

RENDEZVOUS

DO WHAT IS NECESSARY WITH THE HAND
AND ARM TO GUIDE THE WOMAN'S HEAD

KISS HER NECK

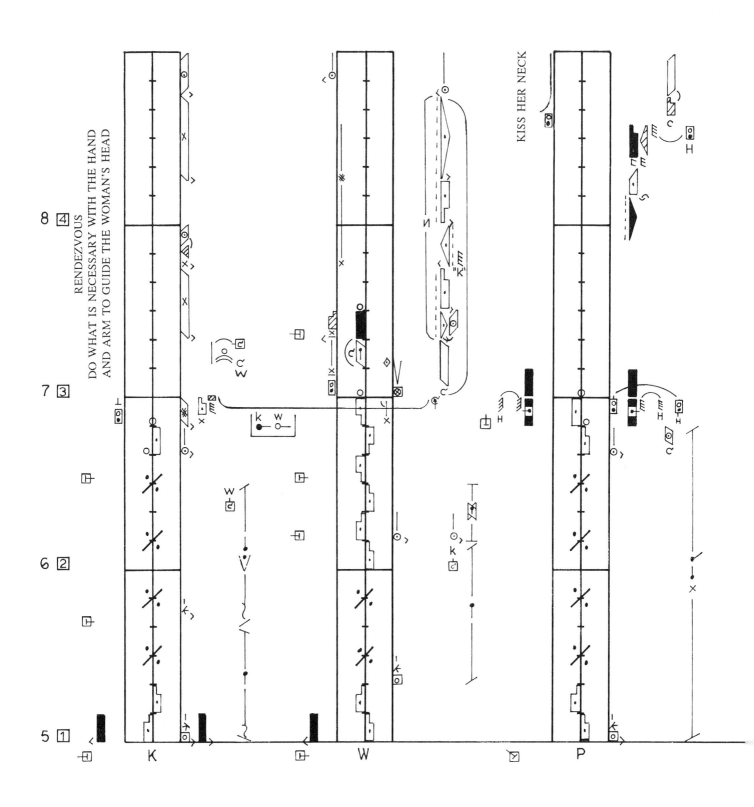

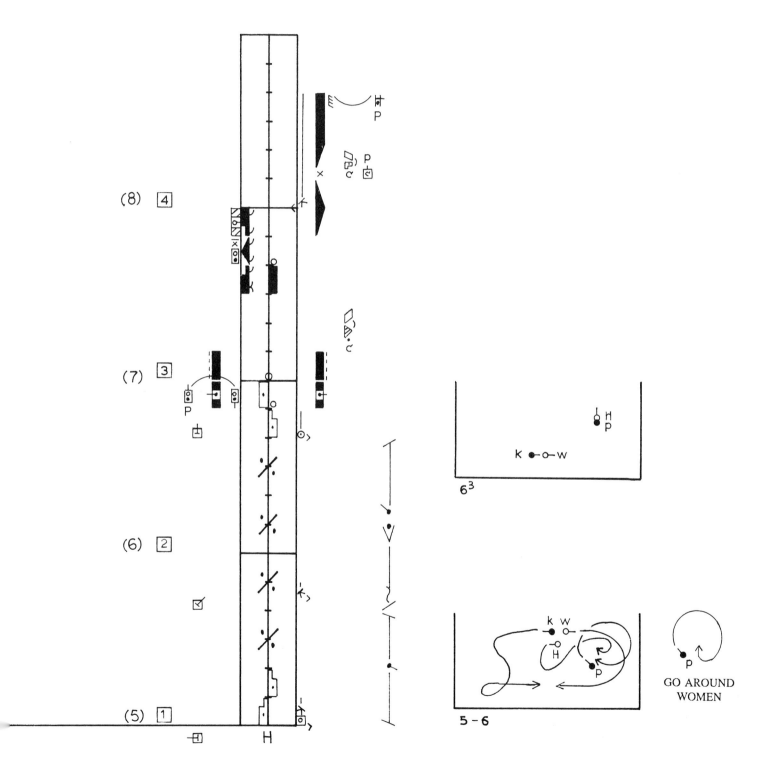

6^3

5 - 6

GO AROUND
WOMEN

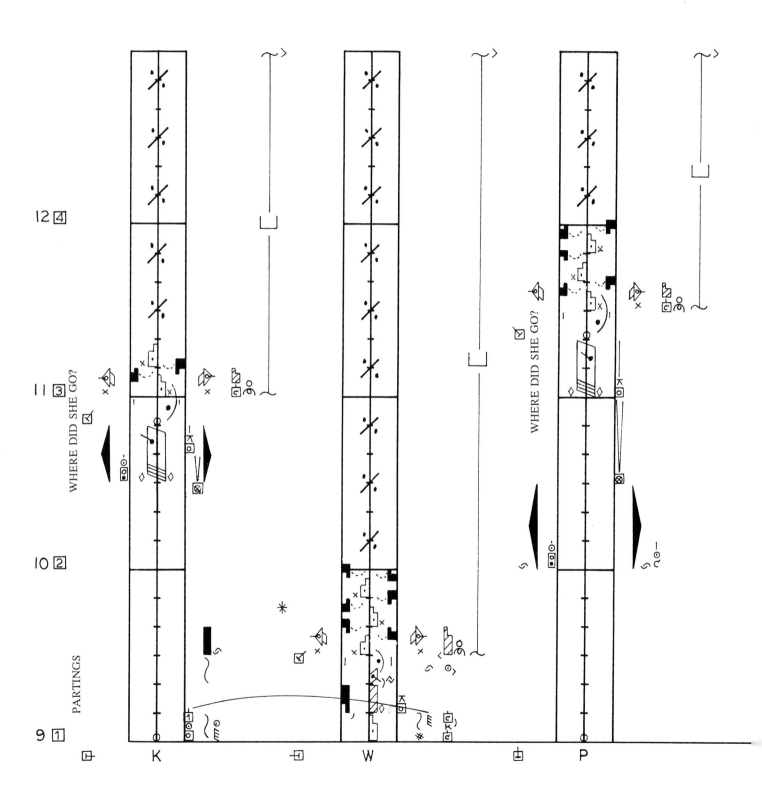

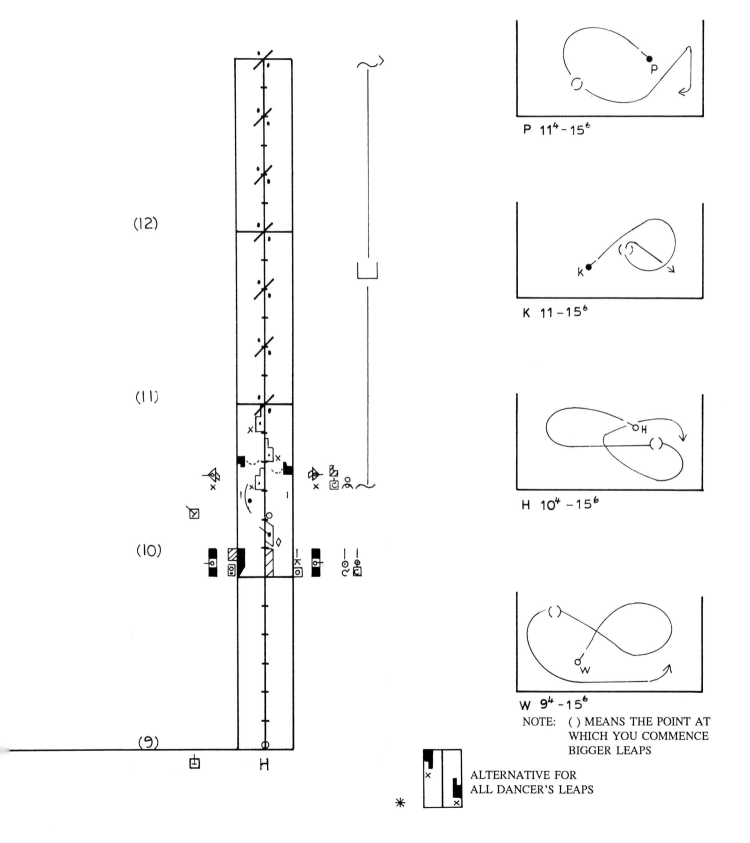

P 11⁴ – 15⁶

K 11 – 15⁶

H 10⁴ – 15⁶

W 9⁴ – 15⁶

NOTE: ( ) MEANS THE POINT AT
WHICH YOU COMMENCE
BIGGER LEAPS

ALTERNATIVE FOR
ALL DANCER'S LEAPS

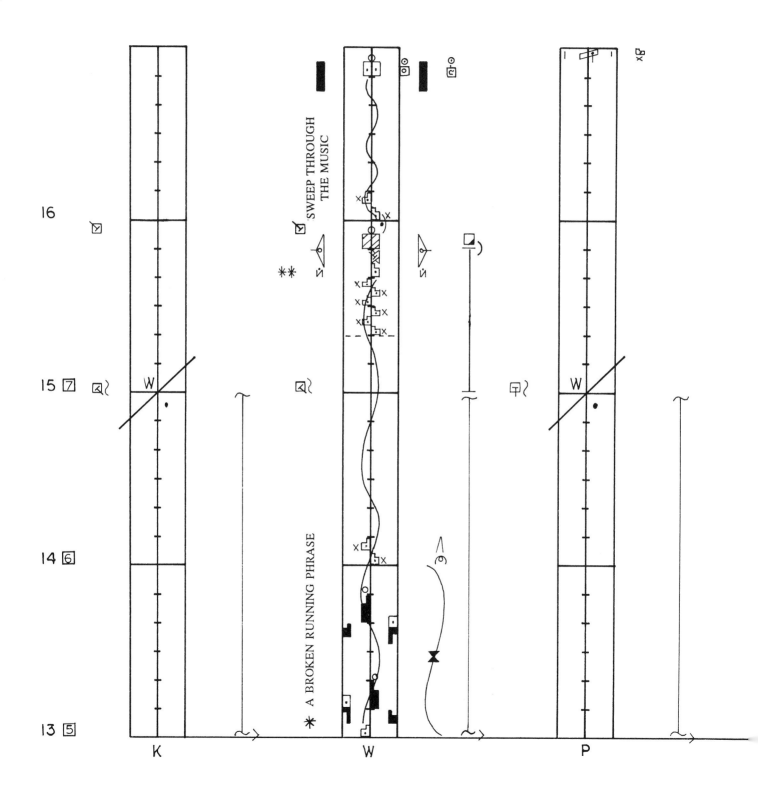

SWEEP THROUGH
THE MUSIC

A BROKEN RUNNING PHRASE

16

15

14

13

K   W   P

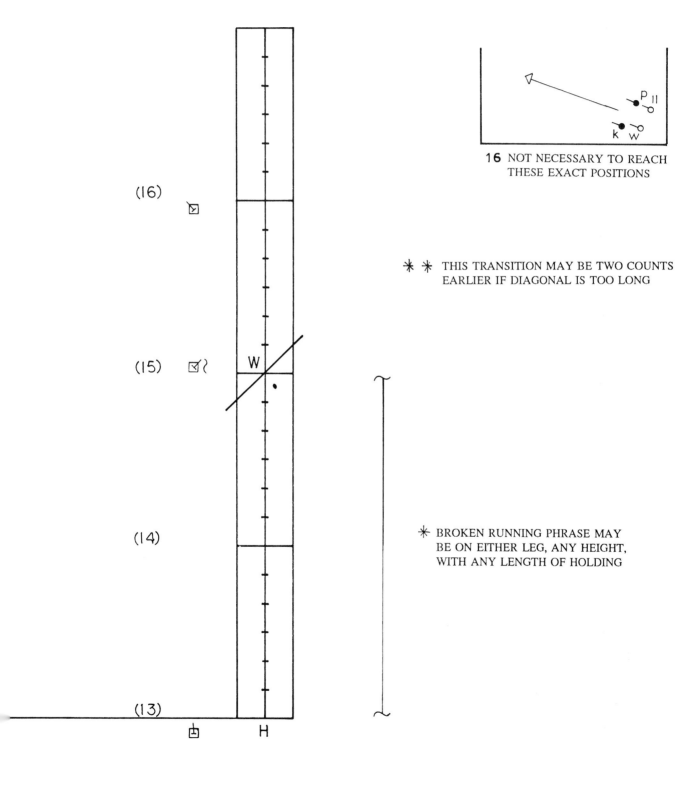

16 NOT NECESSARY TO REACH
THESE EXACT POSITIONS

✳ ✳ THIS TRANSITION MAY BE TWO COUNTS
EARLIER IF DIAGONAL IS TOO LONG

✳ BROKEN RUNNING PHRASE MAY
BE ON EITHER LEG, ANY HEIGHT,
WITH ANY LENGTH OF HOLDING

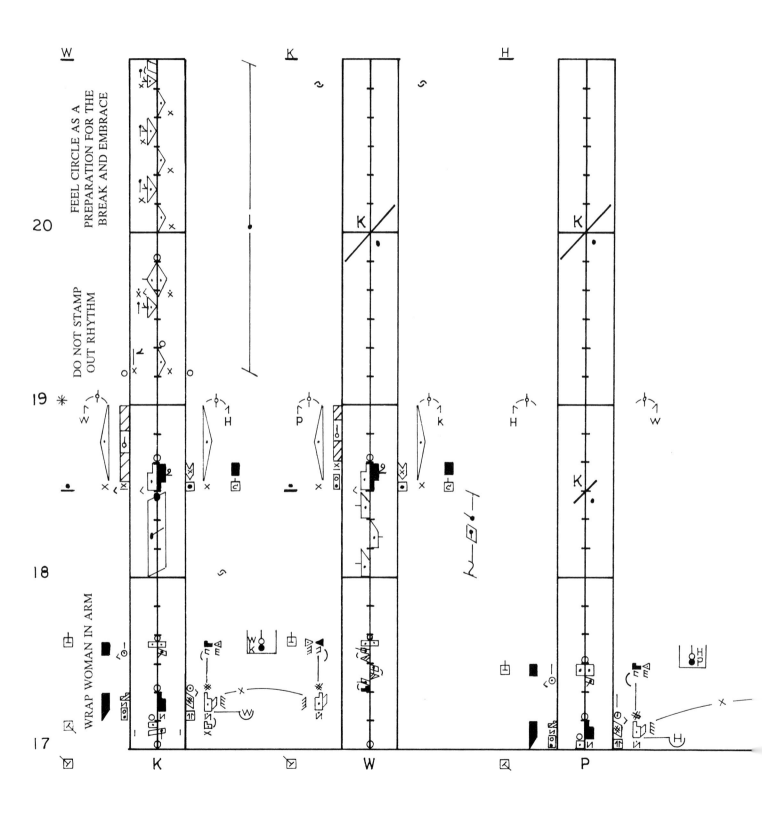

QUARTET
59

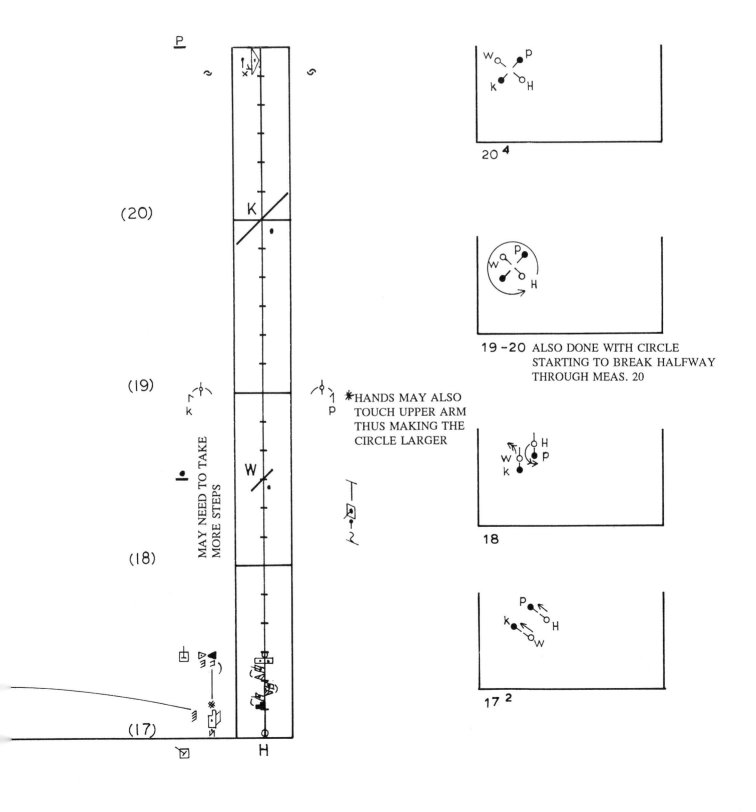

*HANDS MAY ALSO
TOUCH UPPER ARM
THUS MAKING THE
CIRCLE LARGER

MAY NEED TO TAKE
MORE STEPS

19 - 20 ALSO DONE WITH CIRCLE
STARTING TO BREAK HALFWAY
THROUGH MEAS. 20

ALONE

AMOUNT OF TURNING IS UNIMPORTANT. MAN'S ARMS MUST LOOK AS IF THEY
ARE EMBRACING THE WOMAN. THE MAN MAY WALK THROUGH THE MUSIC

STAY WITHIN 'CIRCLE' OF MAN'S ARMS. 'SPOT' EASILY.
MAY DO LESS TURNING BUT STILL STEP ON THE BEAT

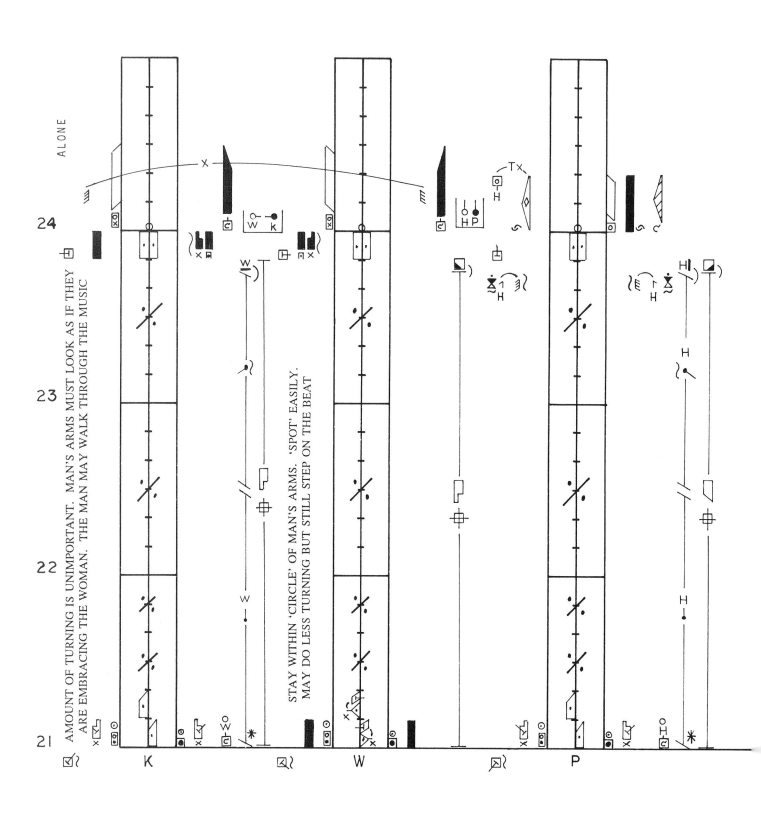

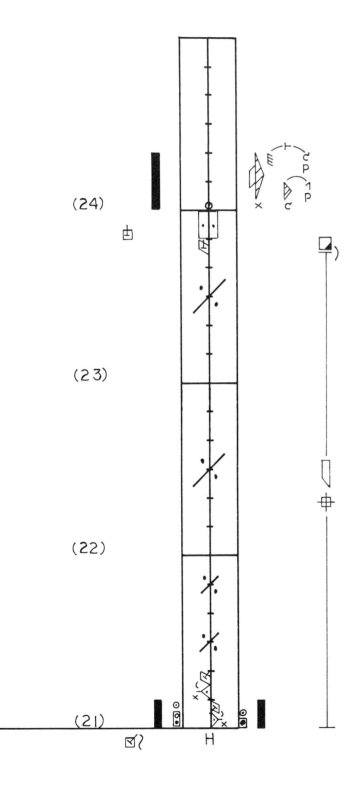

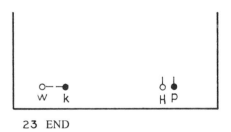

23 END

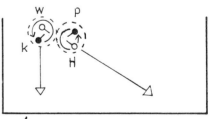

20^4 - 23 APPROXIMATE POSITIONS
AT WHICH TO BREAK

✳ MAN'S PATH AROUND WOMAN NEED NOT BE
A TRUE CIRCLE, BUT MORE ELLIPTICAL. HE
MAY ALSO SLOW DOWN OR SPEED UP AS
NEEDED. ANY ADJUSTMENTS SHOULD NOT
BE ABRUPT, BUT BLENDED.

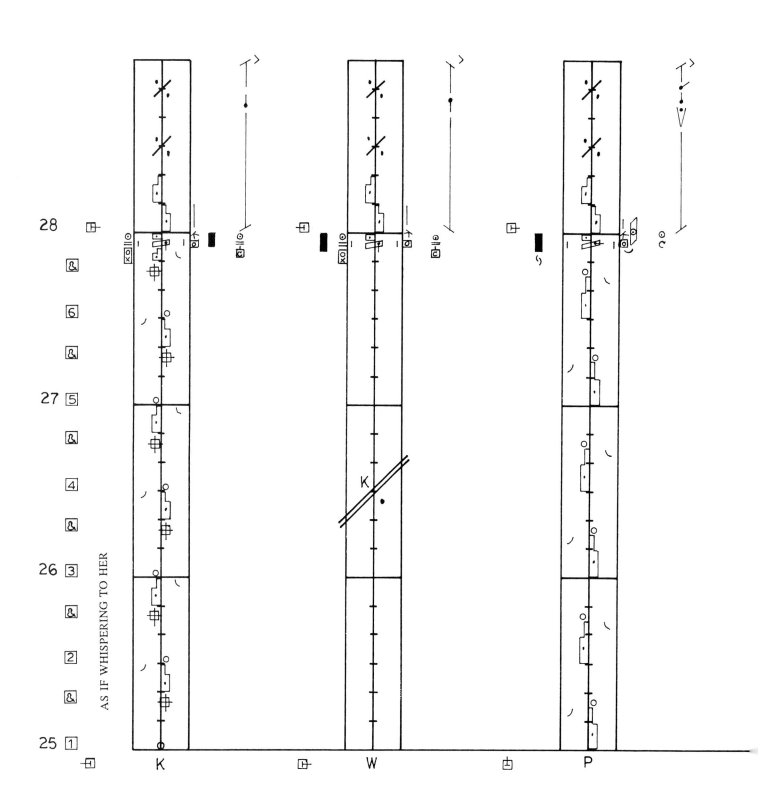

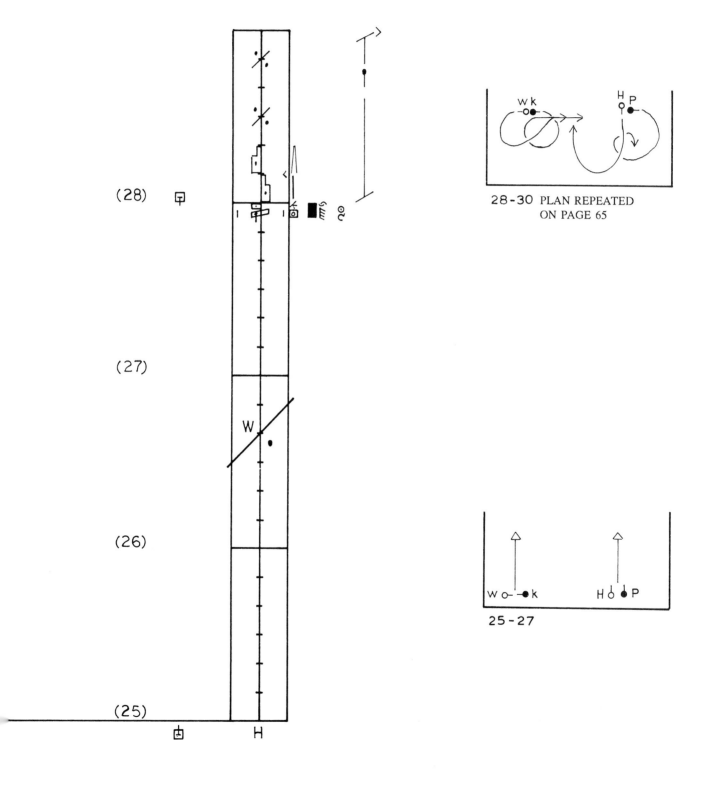

(28)

(27)

(26)

(25)

H

28-30 PLAN REPEATED
ON PAGE 65

25-27

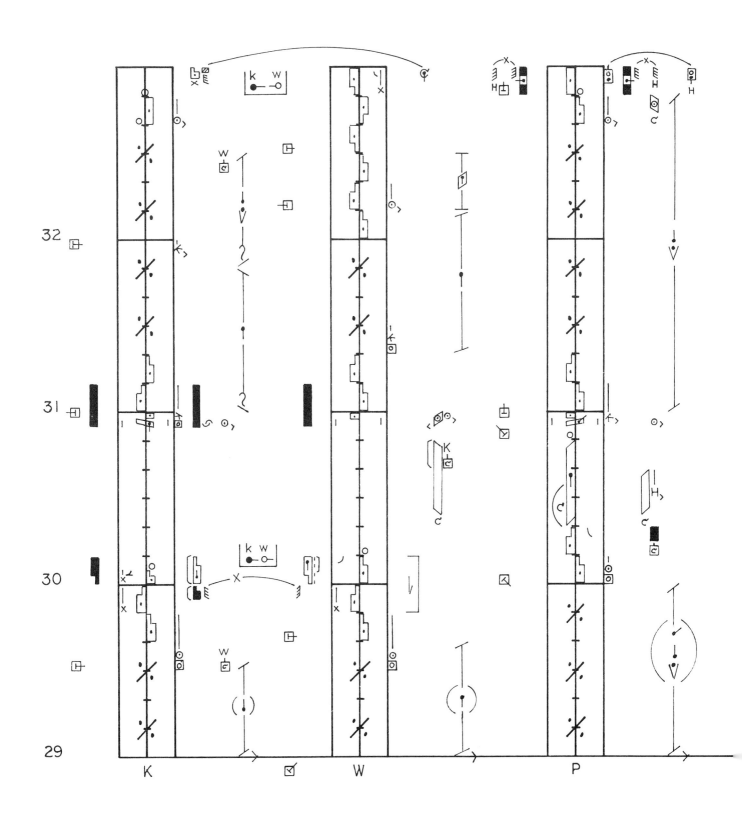

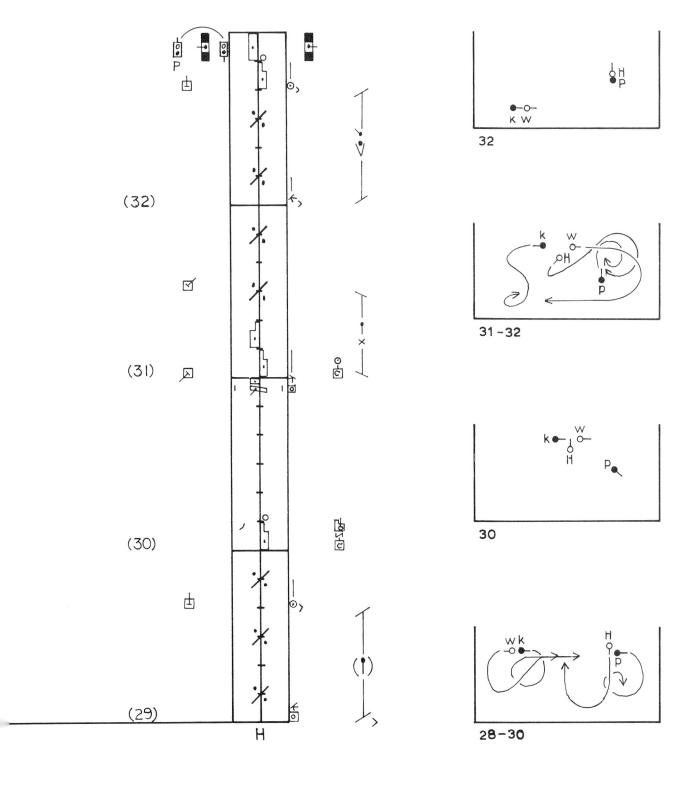

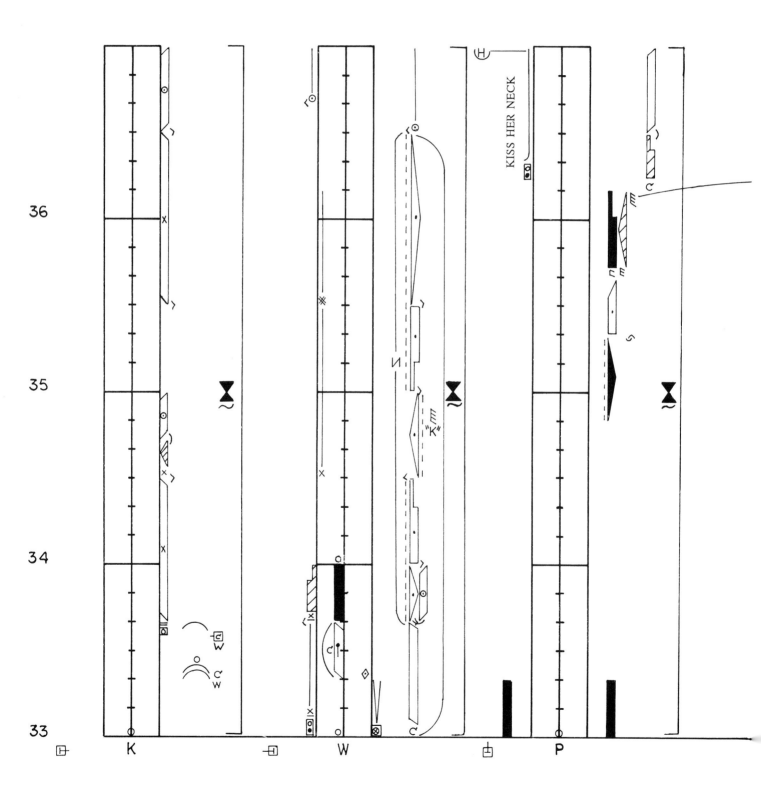

KISS HER NECK

36

35

34

33

K   W   P

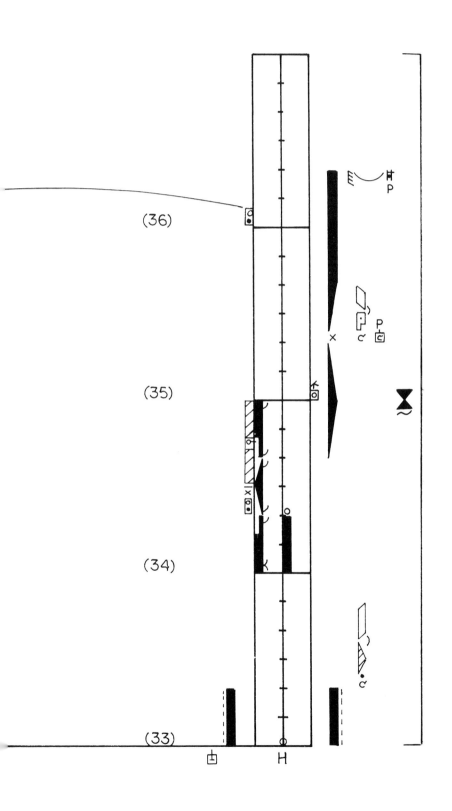

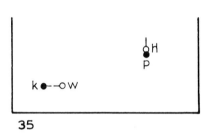

35

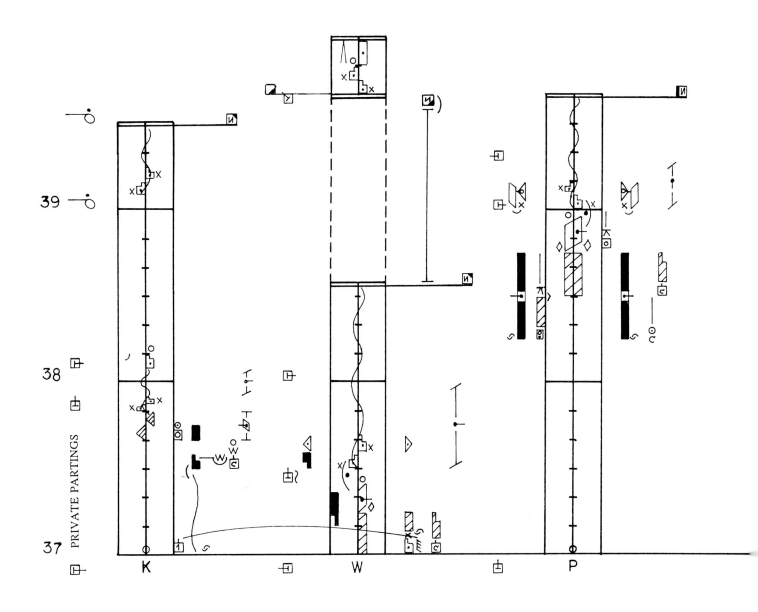

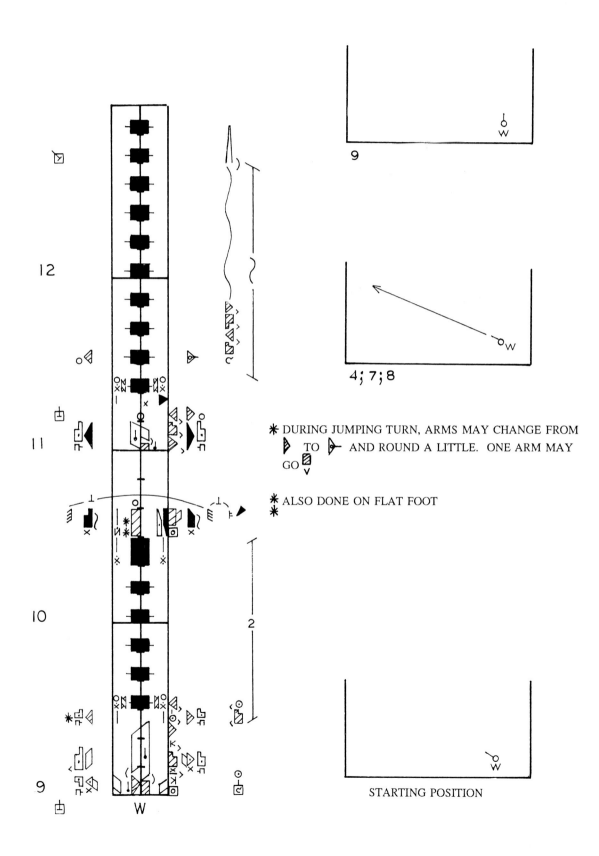

✳ DURING JUMPING TURN, ARMS MAY CHANGE FROM
▷ TO ◁ AND ROUND A LITTLE. ONE ARM MAY
GO ◱

✳✳ ALSO DONE ON FLAT FOOT

9

4; 7; 8

STARTING POSITION

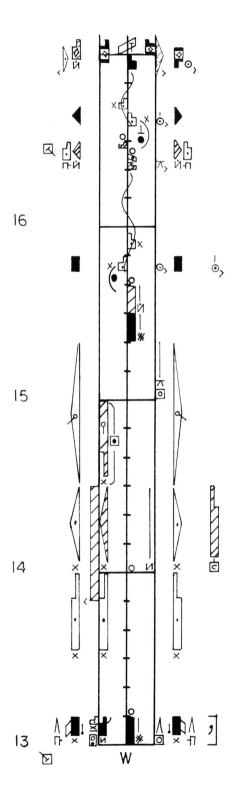

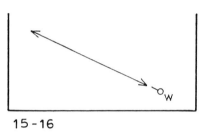

15 - 16

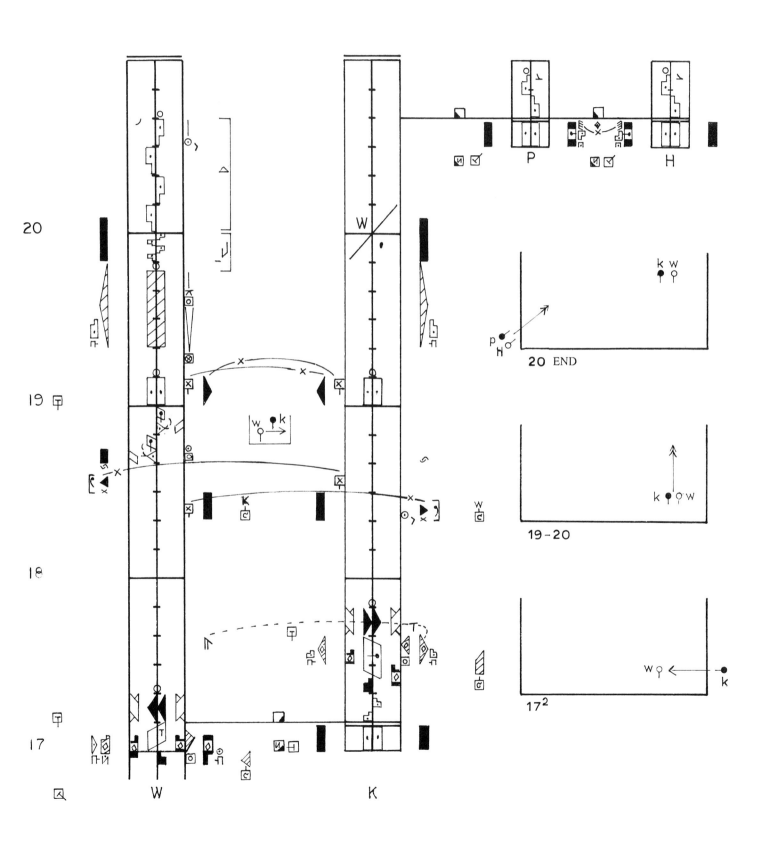

76

(Oleaga)

Ending, interpretation of meas. 52-53
Dennis Nehat and Ze'eva Cohan

POEM: TWO DUETS

78   *BALLADE*

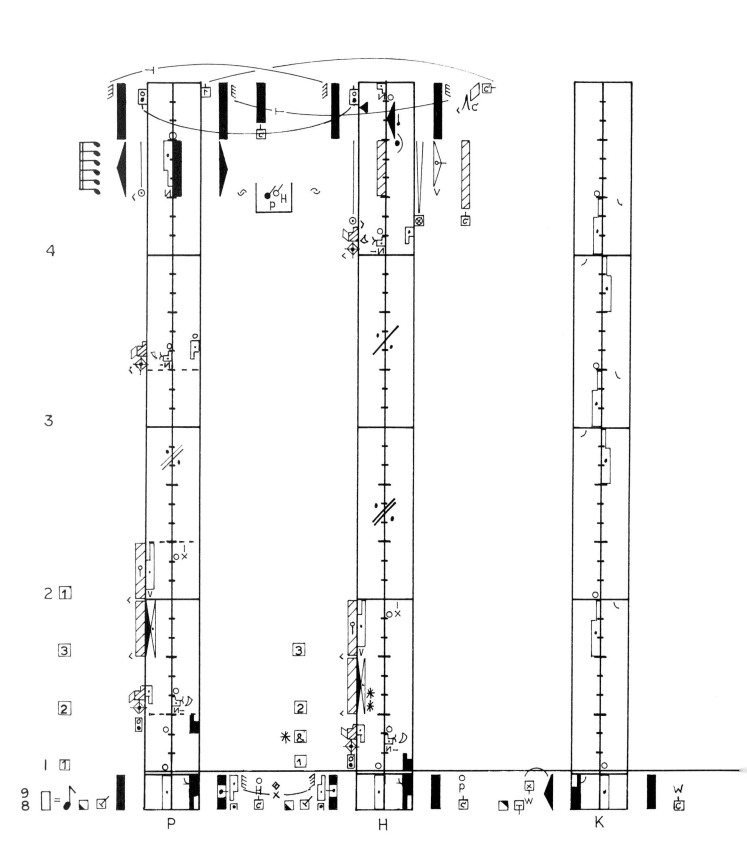

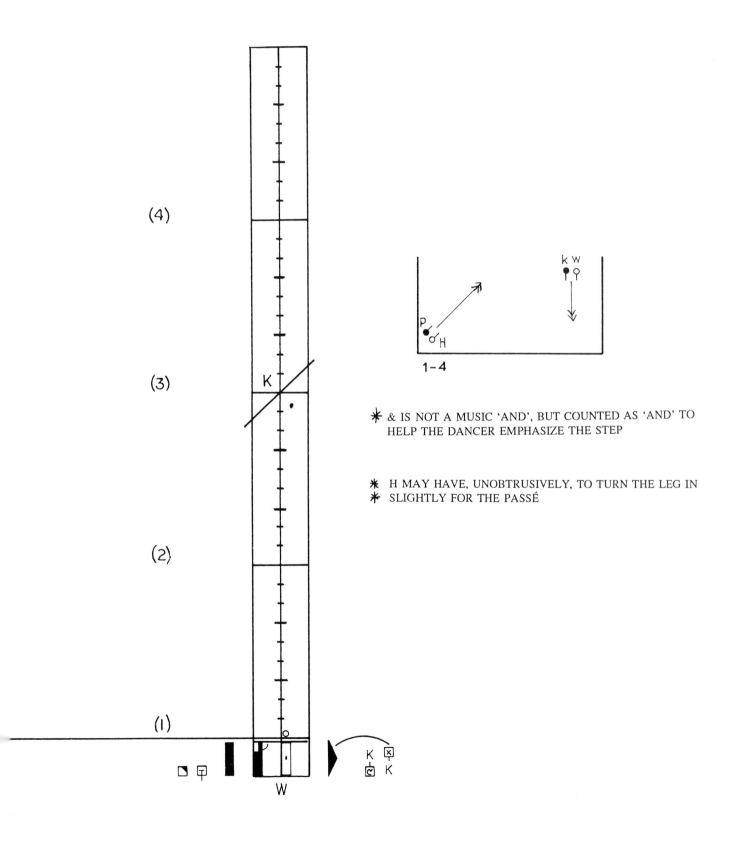

＊ & IS NOT A MUSIC 'AND', BUT COUNTED AS 'AND' TO
   HELP THE DANCER EMPHASIZE THE STEP

＊ H MAY HAVE, UNOBTRUSIVELY, TO TURN THE LEG IN
＊ SLIGHTLY FOR THE PASSÉ

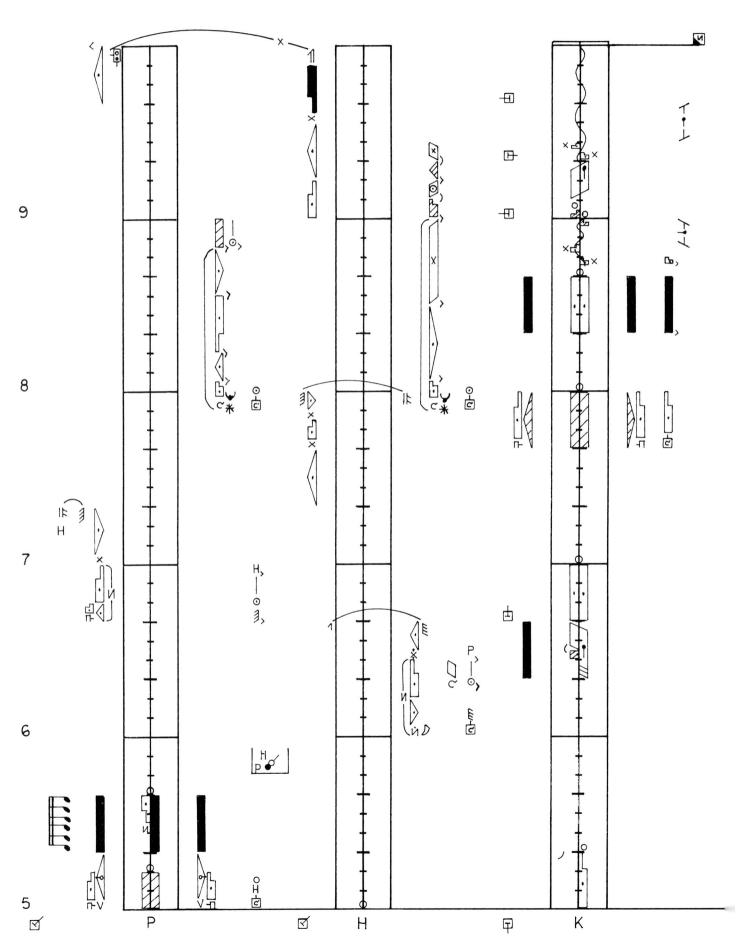

✳ MEAS. 8: EACH DANCER MAKES OWN RHYTHM OF HEAD PHRASE
TO COMPLEMENT ONE ANOTHER

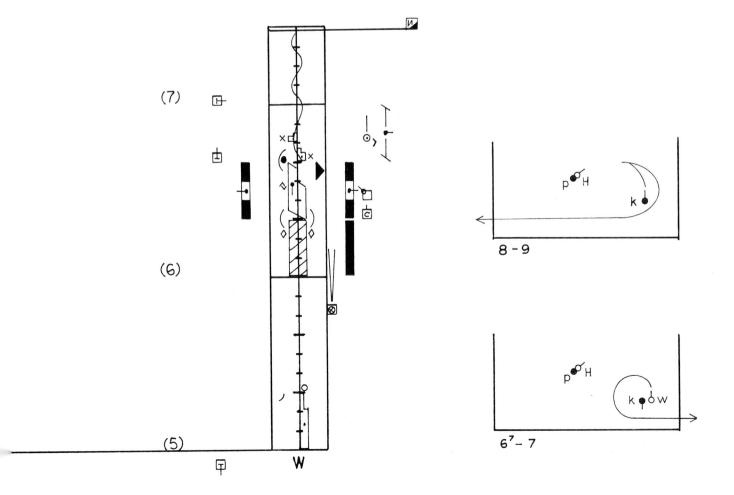

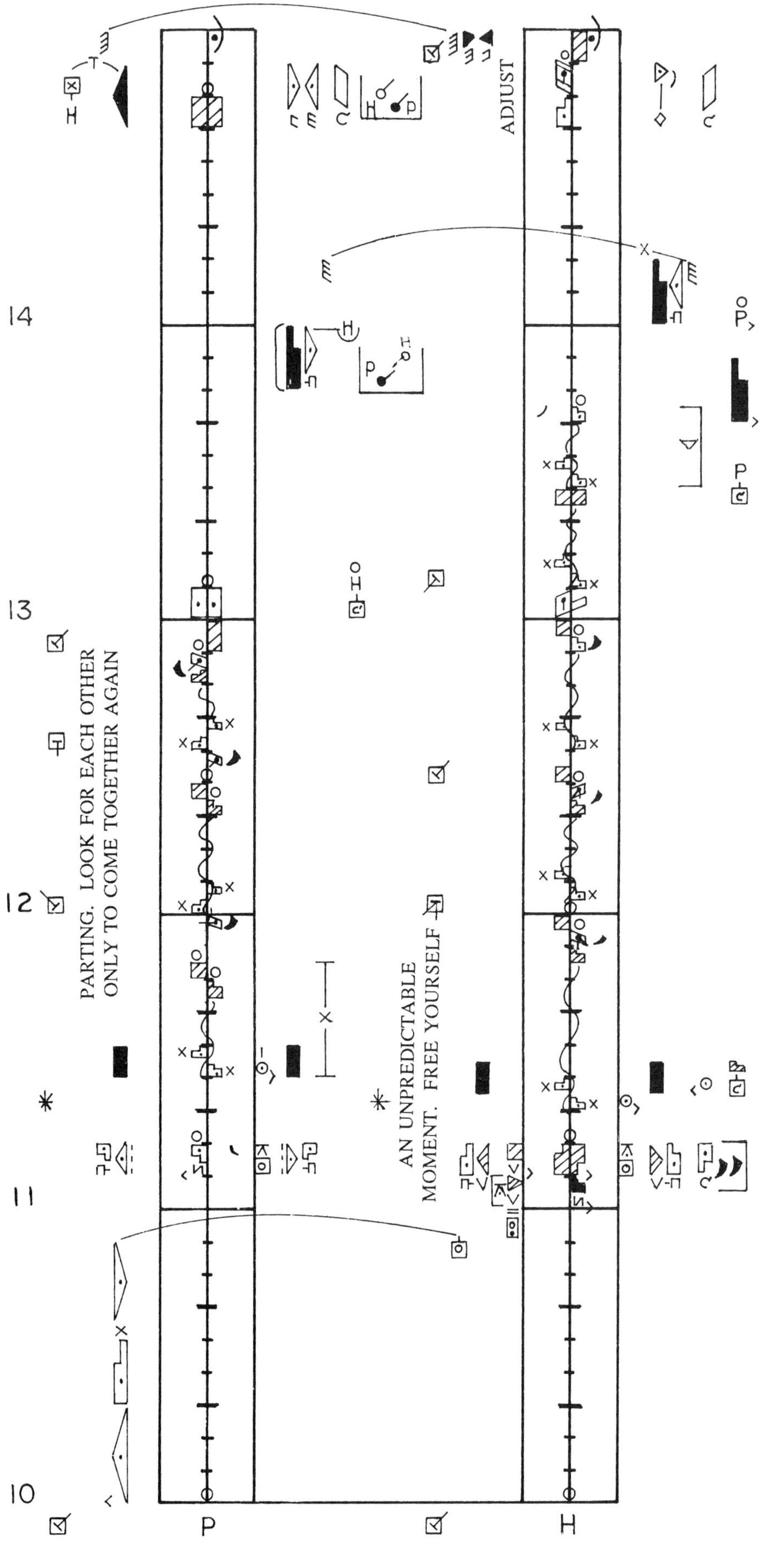

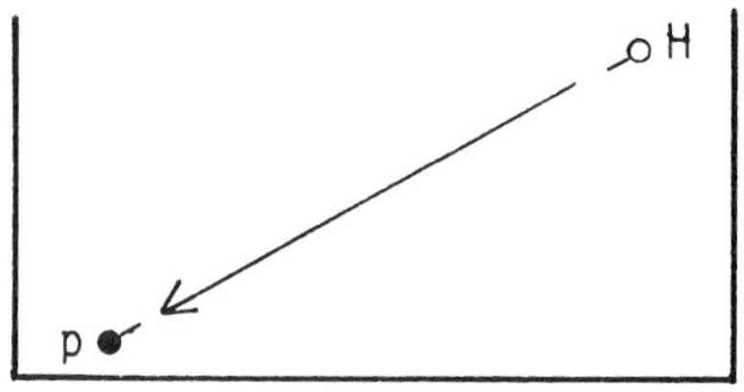

ADJUST

14

13

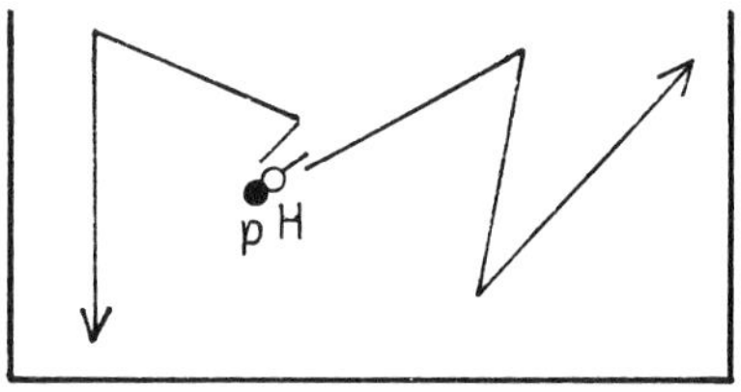

13

12

11

11 - 12

10

P   H

PARTING. LOOK FOR EACH OTHER ONLY TO COME TOGETHER AGAIN

AN UNPREDICTABLE MOMENT. FREE YOURSELF

✳ EACH RUN BUILDS IN ENERGY TO THE MOMENT OF TURN. PATHS, PAUSES AND TURNS SHOULD LOOK UNPLANNED

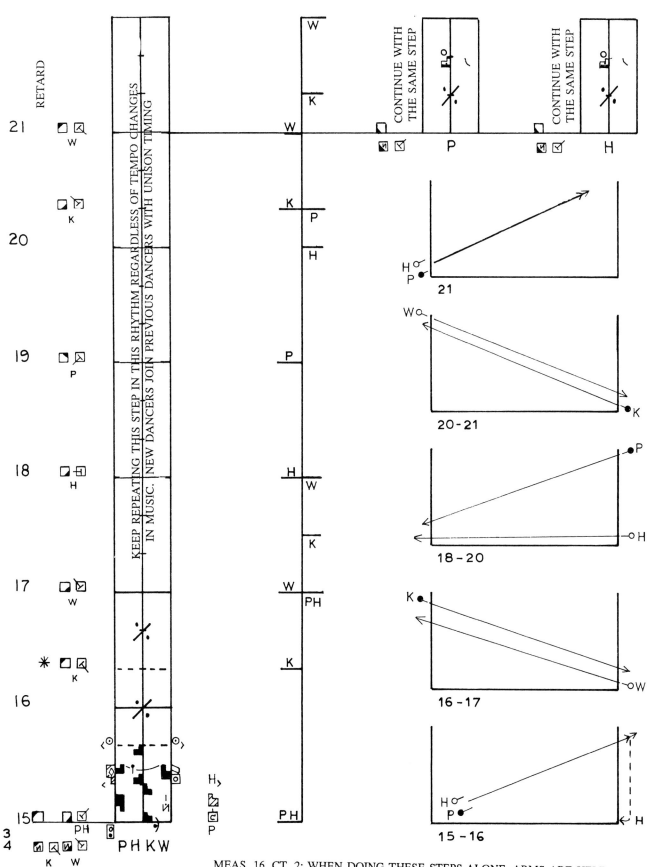

21

20-21

18-20

16-17

15-16

MEAS. 16, CT. 2: WHEN DOING THESE STEPS ALONE, ARMS ARE HELD
IN SECOND POSITION AND YOU MAY START ON EITHER FOOT.
HEAD MAY TILT TO LEFT ON CHEST ROTATION. FOCUS
MAY LOOK TO LEFT.

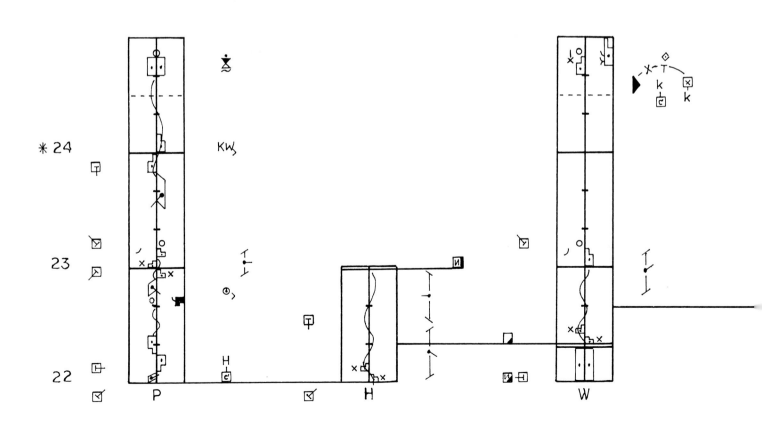

84   *BALLADE*

MEAS. 24:   THIS WILL BE REPEATED ON PAGE 86 FOR W, K, P. THE NEW DANCE PHRASE
                  COMMENCES AT THE DOTTED LINE

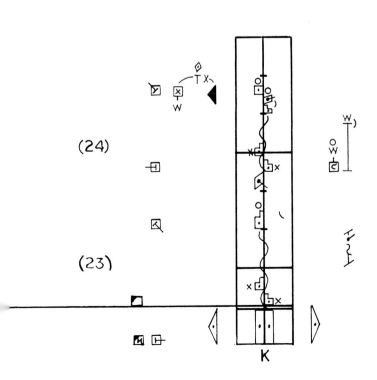

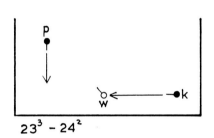

$23^3 - 24^2$

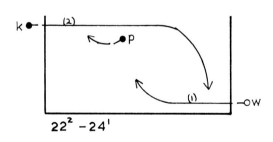

$22^2 - 24^1$

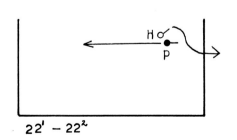

$22^1 - 22^2$

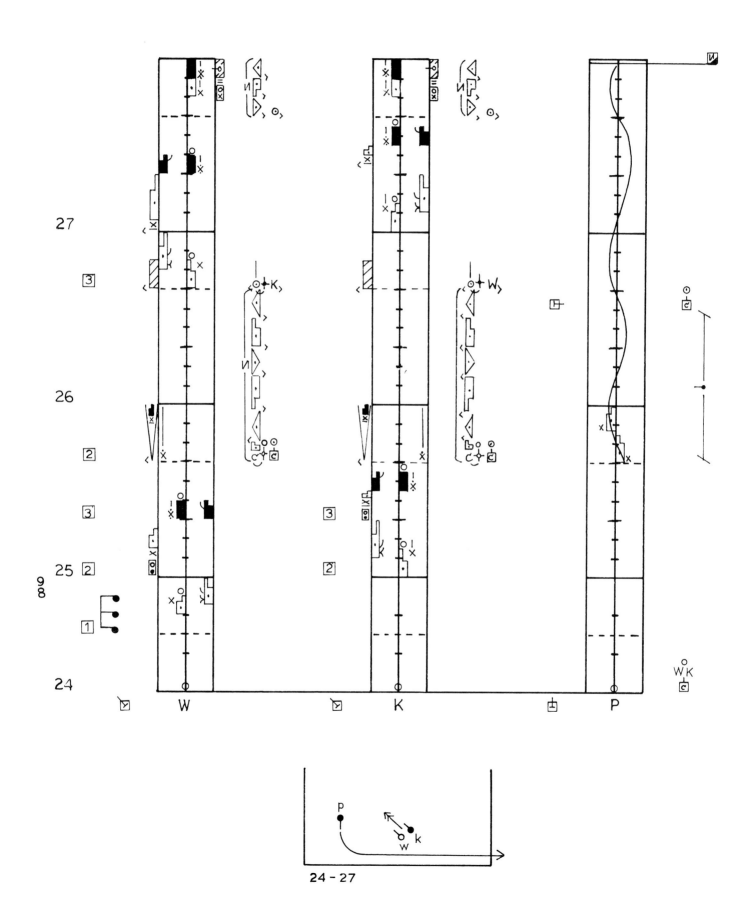

24 - 27

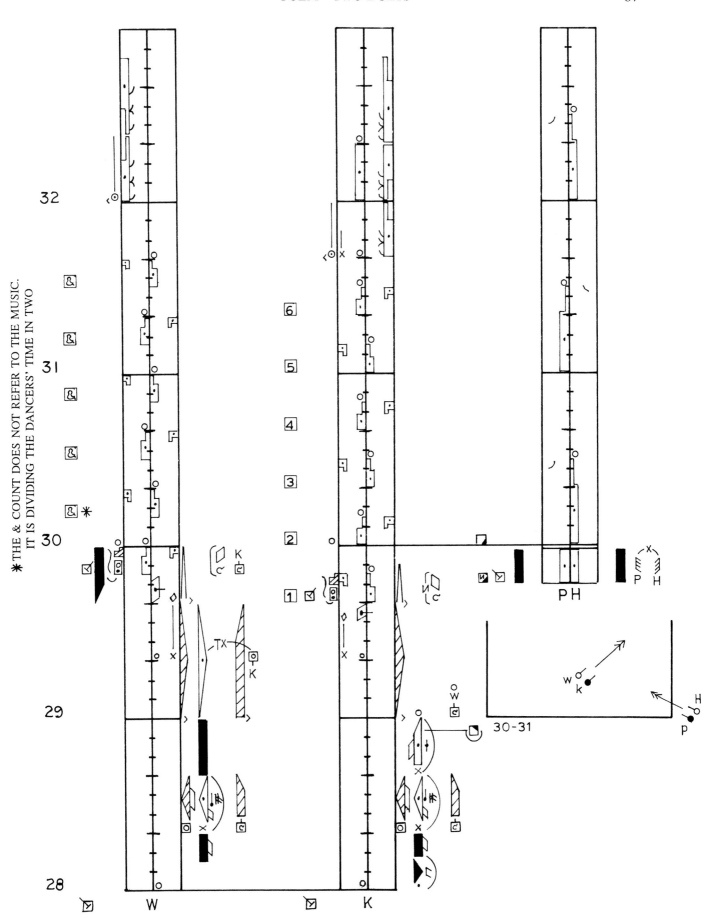

**THE & COUNT DOES NOT REFER TO THE MUSIC. IT IS DIVIDING THE DANCERS' TIME IN TWO

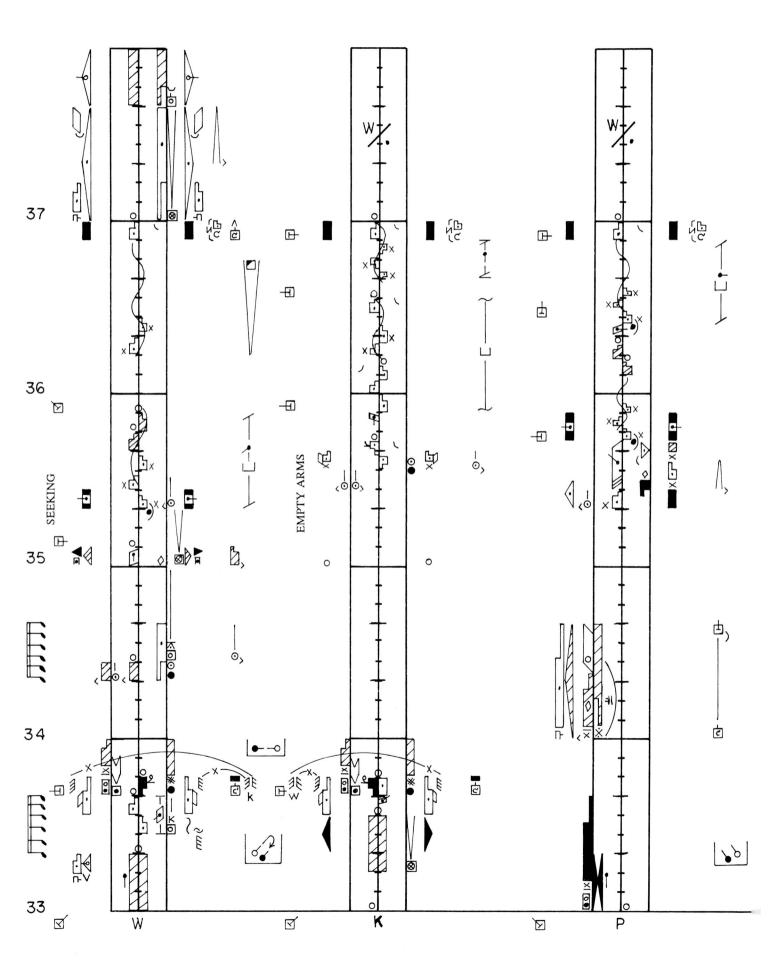

SEEKING

EMPTY ARMS

37

36

35

34

33

W

K

P

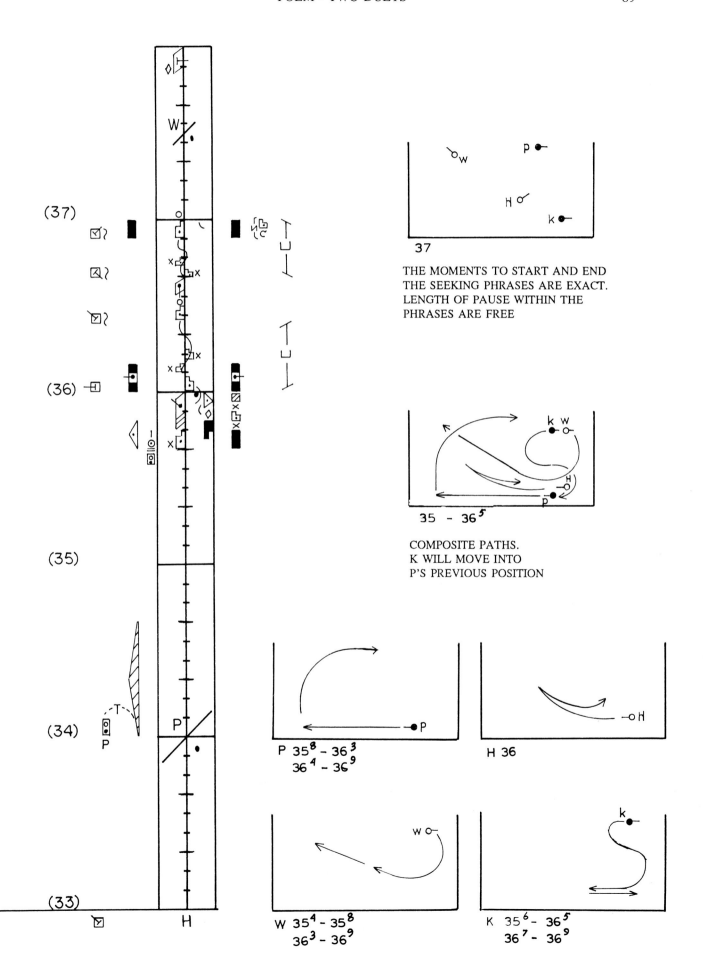

THE MOMENTS TO START AND END
THE SEEKING PHRASES ARE EXACT.
LENGTH OF PAUSE WITHIN THE
PHRASES ARE FREE

35 - 36⁵

COMPOSITE PATHS.
K WILL MOVE INTO
P'S PREVIOUS POSITION

P 35⁸ - 36³
36⁴ - 36⁹

H 36

W 35⁴ - 35⁸
36³ - 36⁹

K 35⁶ - 36⁵
36⁷ - 36⁹

MEAS. 39-44:   LOVERS RUNNING THROUGH THE WOODS
                  ONLY TO MISS ONE ANOTHER. ALL RUNS,
                  LEAPS, CHASSÉ TURNS MAY BE ON EITHER
                  LEG. ALL LEAPS ARE AS HIGH AS POSSIBLE
                  AND OCCUR CLOSE TO THE WING OF THE
                  EXIT. ENTRANCE TIME IS EXACT, EXIT TIME
                  DEPENDS ON SIZE OF STAGE. ENTRANCES
                  AND EXITS MUST OVERLAP. ALL
                  MOVEMENT SHOULD BE LARGE AND FREE.

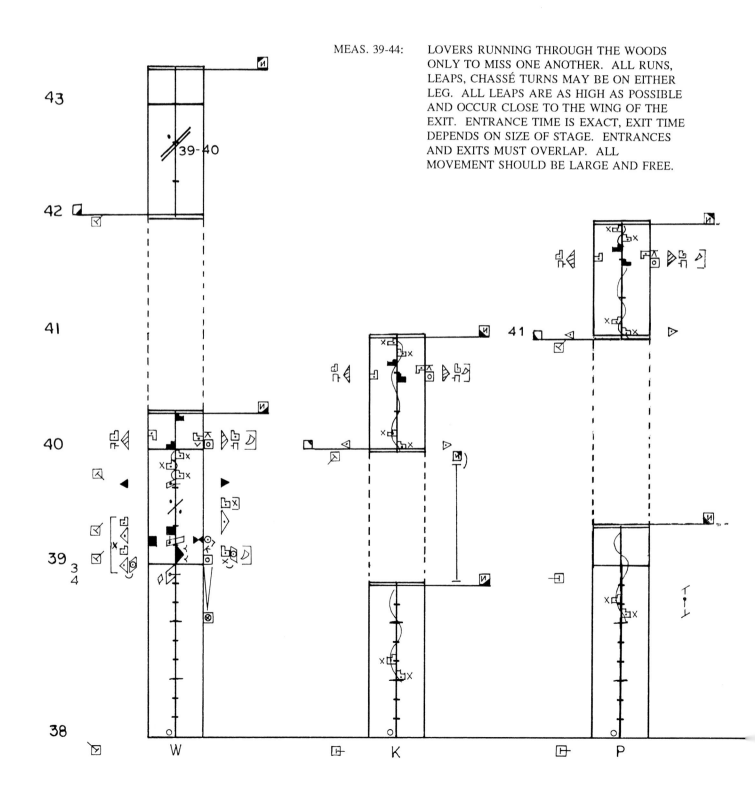

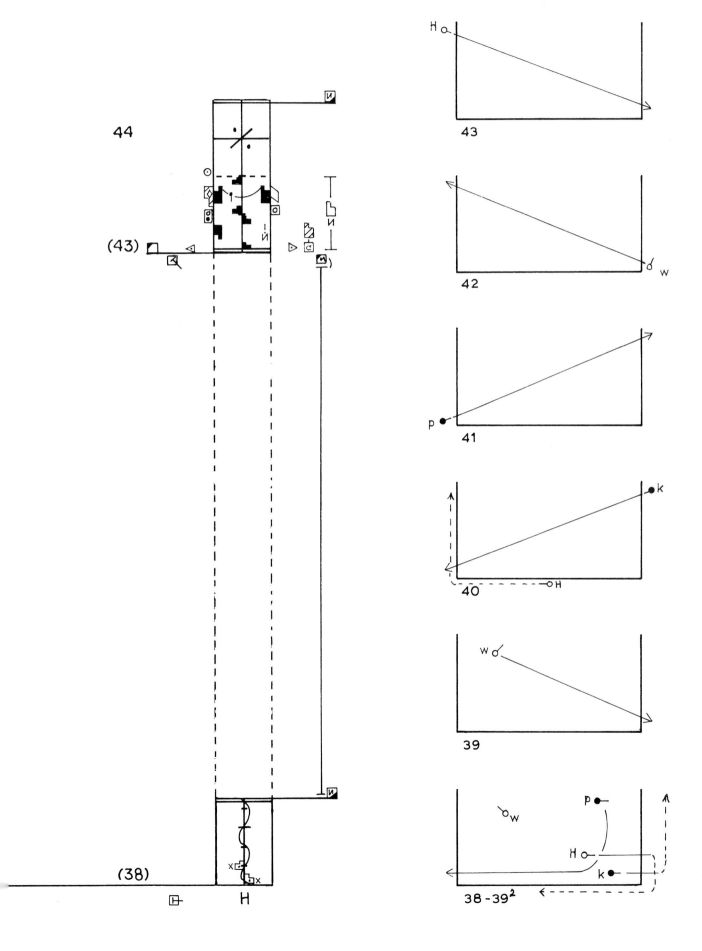

43

42

41

40

39

38 - 39^2

44

(43)

(38)

H

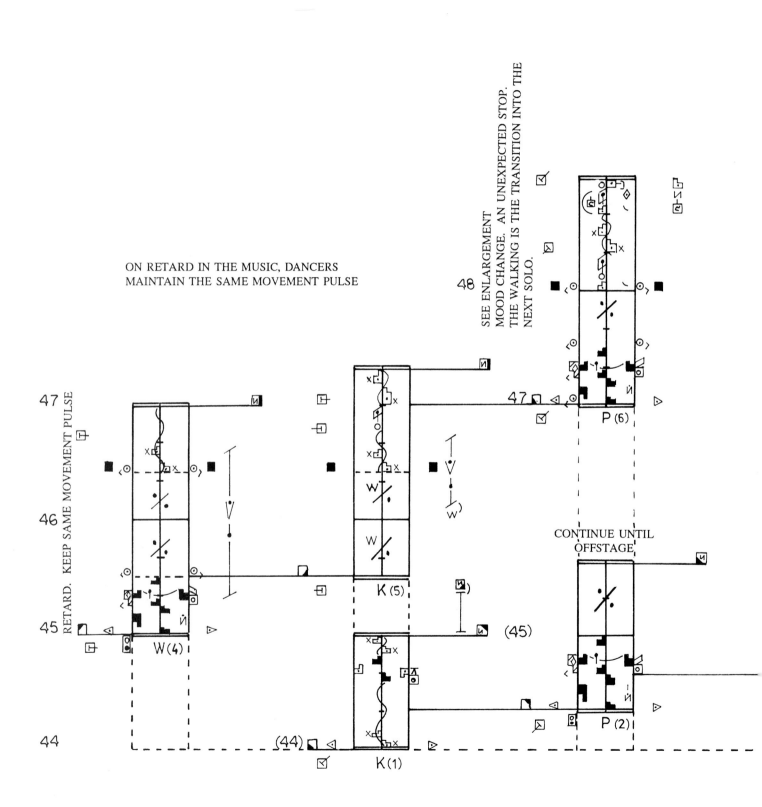

ON RETARD IN THE MUSIC, DANCERS
MAINTAIN THE SAME MOVEMENT PULSE

SEE ENLARGEMENT
MOOD CHANGE. AN UNEXPECTED STOP.
THE WALKING IS THE TRANSITION INTO THE
NEXT SOLO.

RETARD. KEEP SAME MOVEMENT PULSE

CONTINUE UNTIL
OFFSTAGE

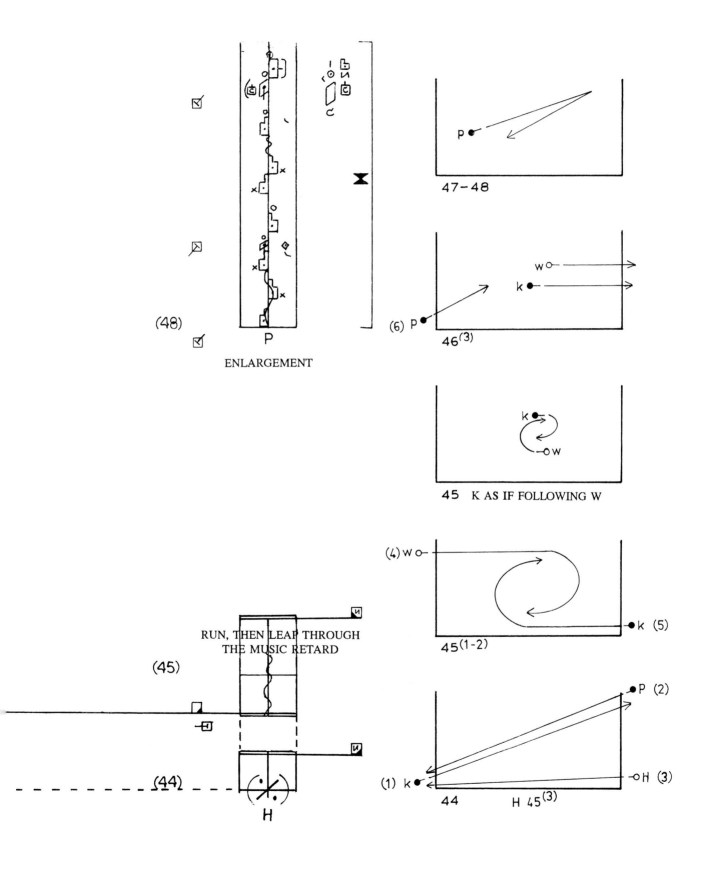

(48)

P

ENLARGEMENT

47-48

(6) P   46⁽³⁾   w   k

45   K AS IF FOLLOWING W

(4) w   k (5)   45⁽¹⁻²⁾

(45)   RUN, THEN LEAP THROUGH
THE MUSIC RETARD

(44)   H

P (2)   (1) k   H (3)   44   H 45⁽³⁾

94

Opening Continued, meas. 18
Jim May

(David Fullard)

MAN'S SOLO

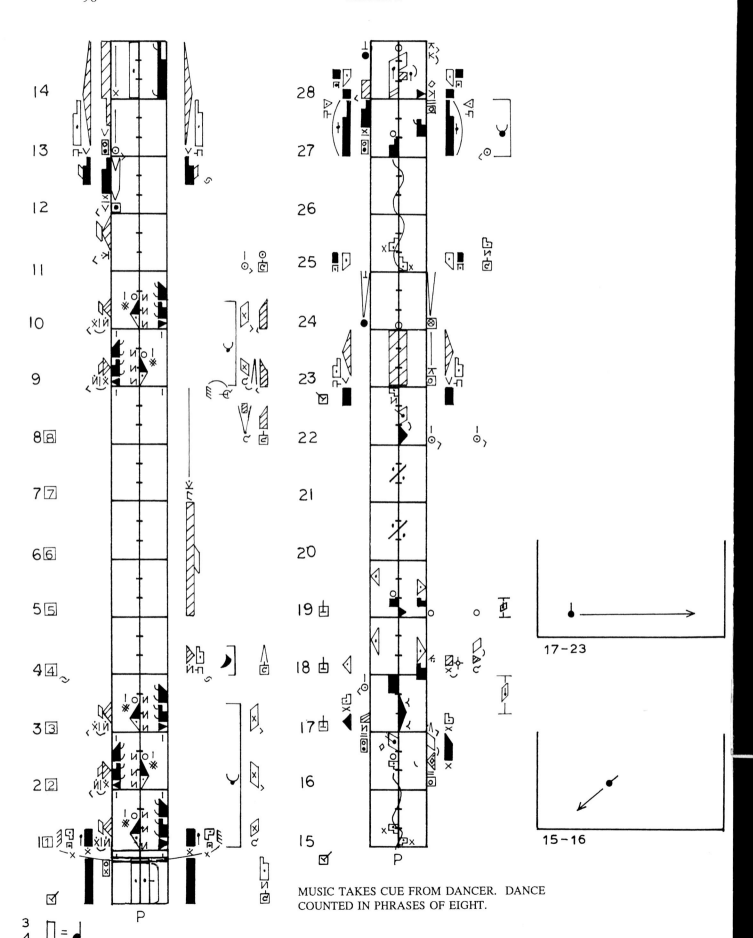

96   *BALLADE*

MUSIC TAKES CUE FROM DANCER. DANCE
COUNTED IN PHRASES OF EIGHT.

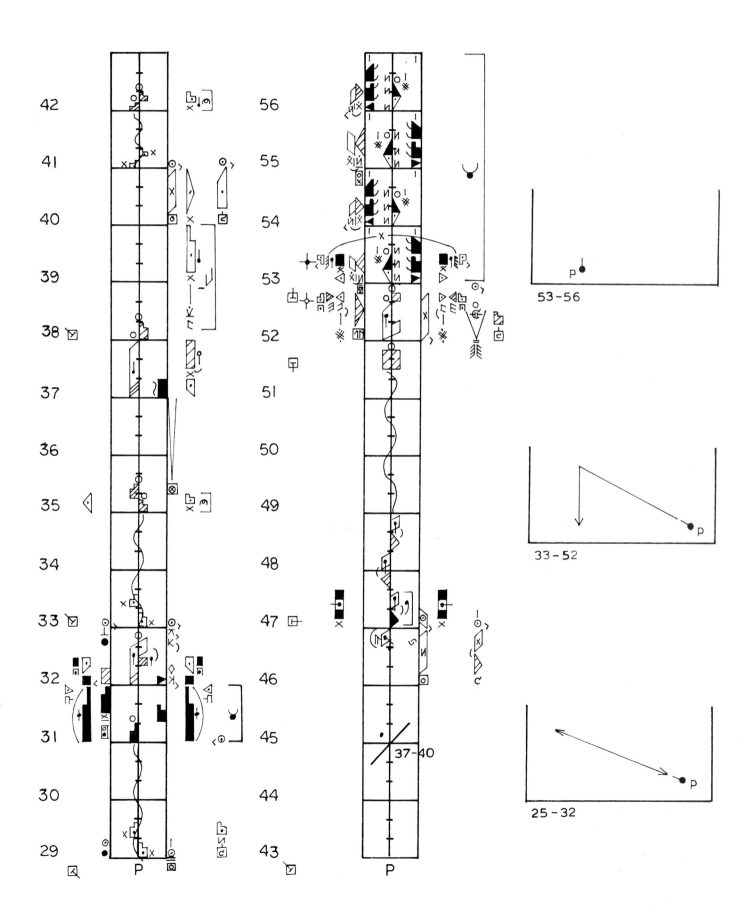

53-56

33-52

37-40

25-32

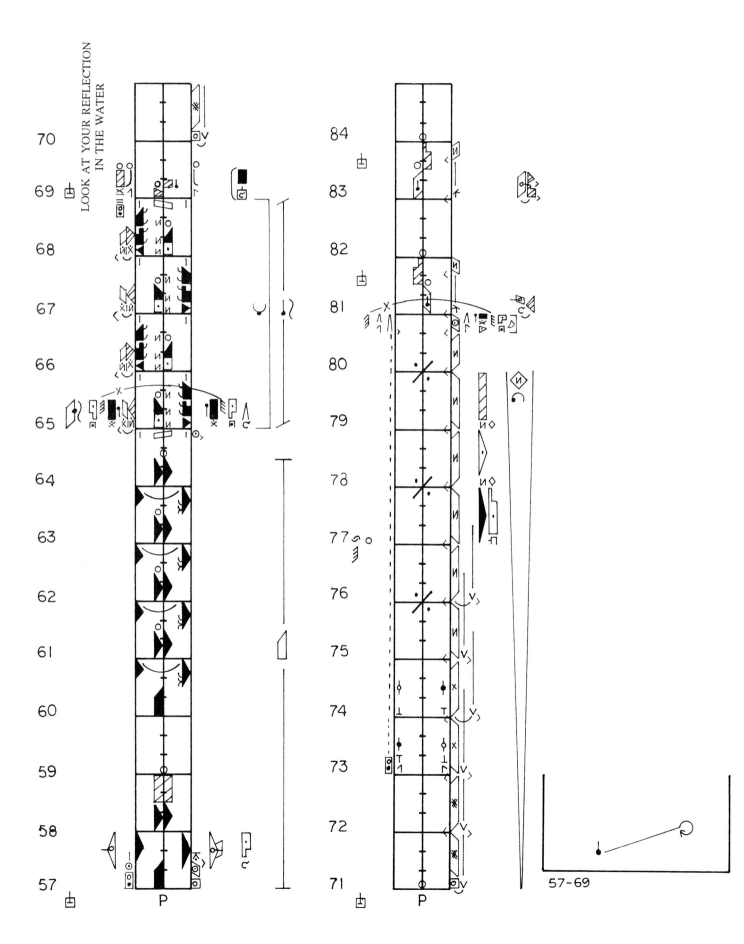

LOOK AT YOUR REFLECTION IN THE WATER

57–69

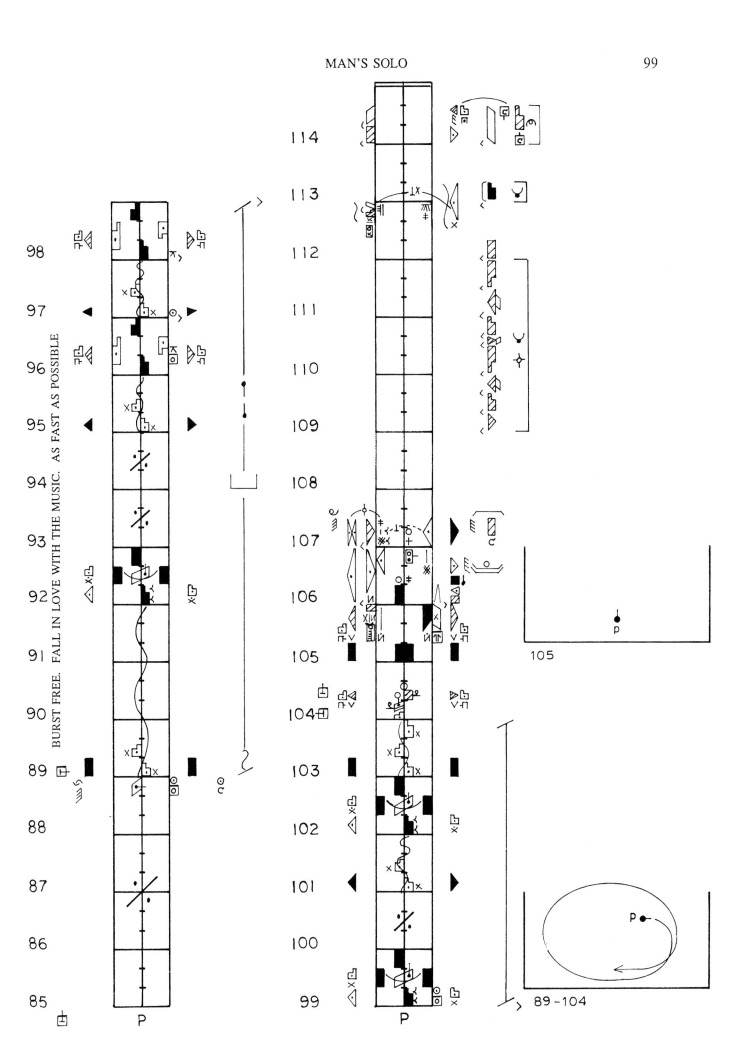

BURST FREE. FALL IN LOVE WITH THE MUSIC. AS FAST AS POSSIBLE

100

Poem - Two Duets, meas. 15
Marc Stevens and Mary Margaret Giannone

ENDING

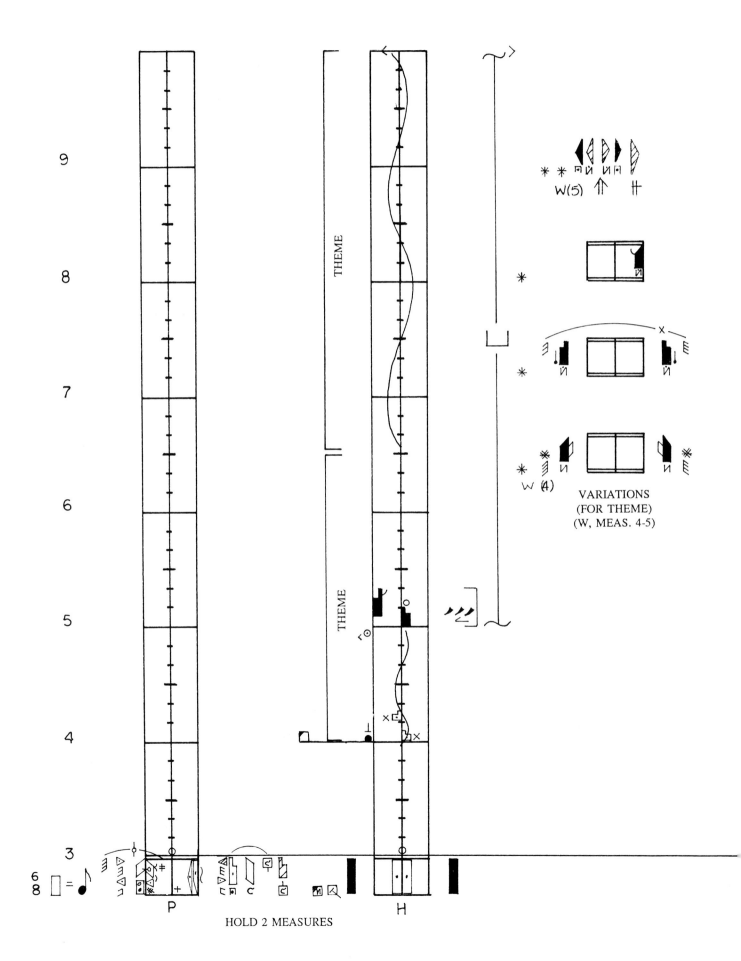

THEME

THEME

VARIATIONS
(FOR THEME)
(W, MEAS. 4-5)

W(5)

W (4)

9

8

7

6

5

4

3

6
8

P

H

HOLD 2 MEASURES

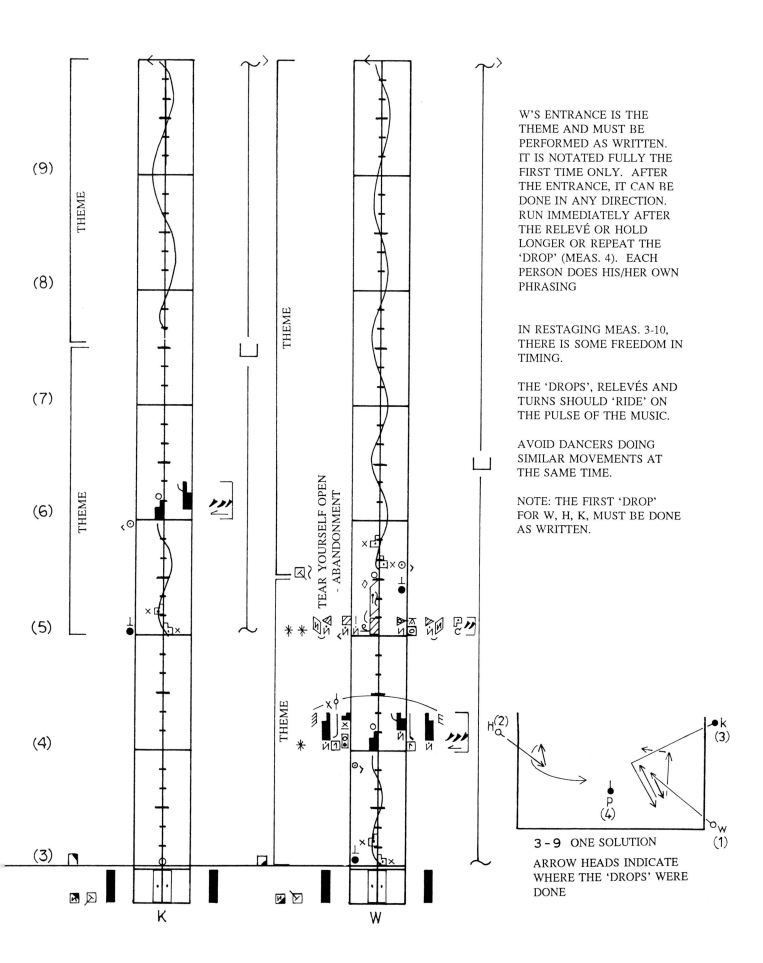

W'S ENTRANCE IS THE
THEME AND MUST BE
PERFORMED AS WRITTEN.
IT IS NOTATED FULLY THE
FIRST TIME ONLY. AFTER
THE ENTRANCE, IT CAN BE
DONE IN ANY DIRECTION.
RUN IMMEDIATELY AFTER
THE RELEVÉ OR HOLD
LONGER OR REPEAT THE
'DROP' (MEAS. 4). EACH
PERSON DOES HIS/HER OWN
PHRASING

IN RESTAGING MEAS. 3-10,
THERE IS SOME FREEDOM IN
TIMING.

THE 'DROPS', RELEVÉS AND
TURNS SHOULD 'RIDE' ON
THE PULSE OF THE MUSIC.

AVOID DANCERS DOING
SIMILAR MOVEMENTS AT
THE SAME TIME.

NOTE: THE FIRST 'DROP'
FOR W, H, K, MUST BE DONE
AS WRITTEN.

3-9 ONE SOLUTION

ARROW HEADS INDICATE
WHERE THE 'DROPS' WERE
DONE

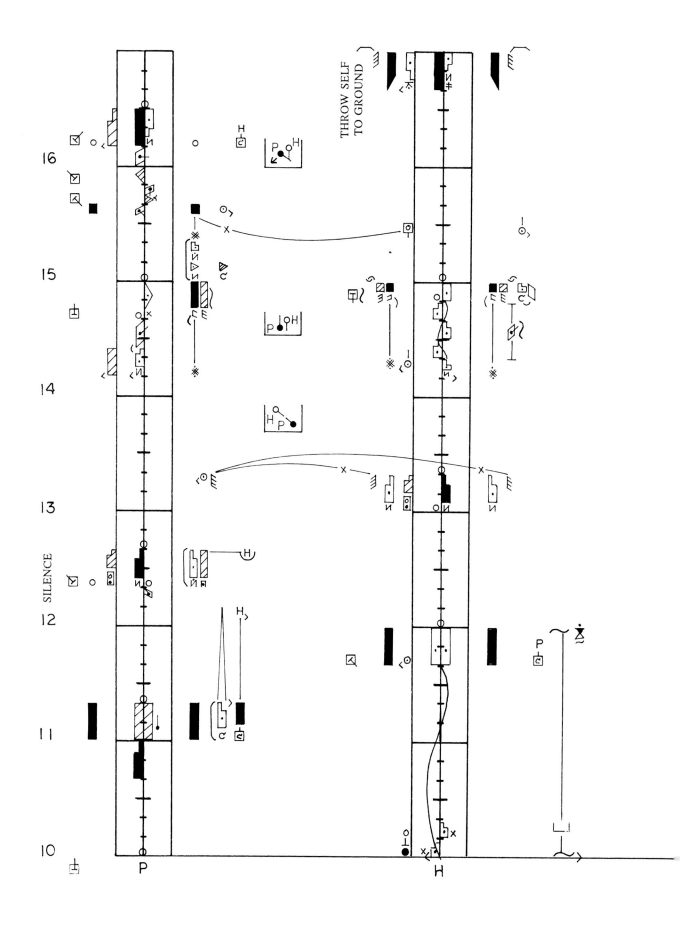

THROW SELF
TO GROUND

SILENCE

16

15

14

13

12

11

10

P

H

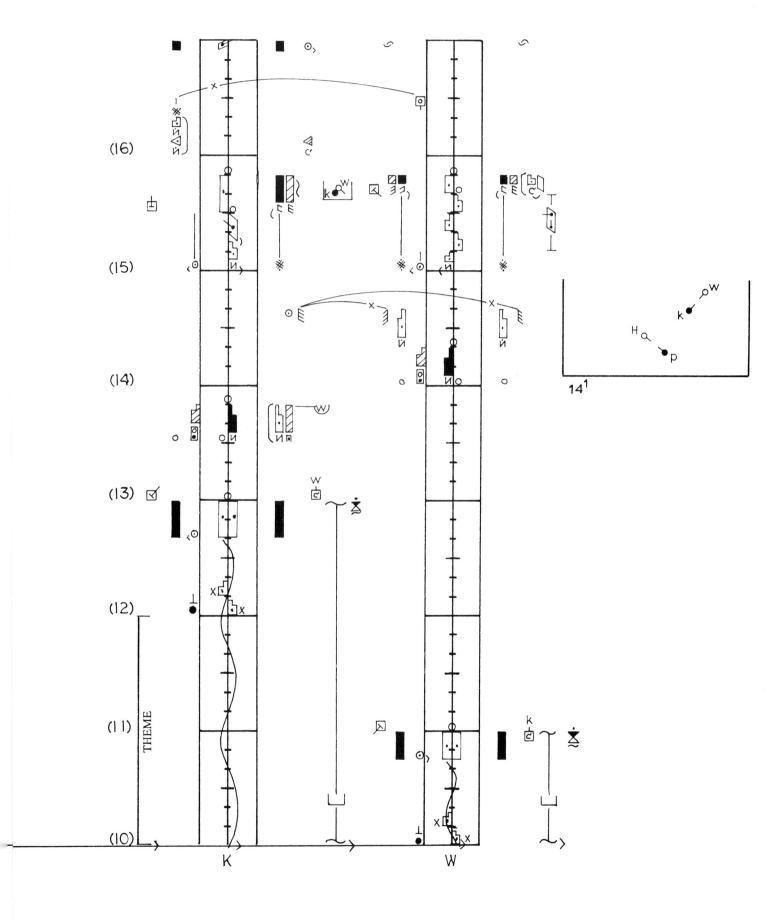

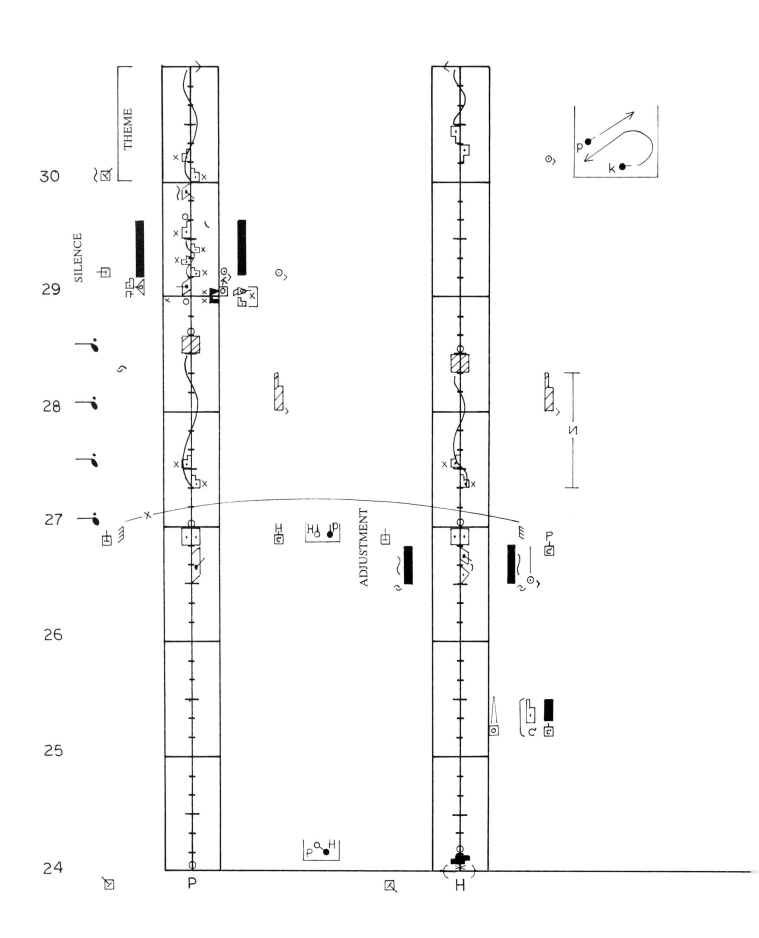

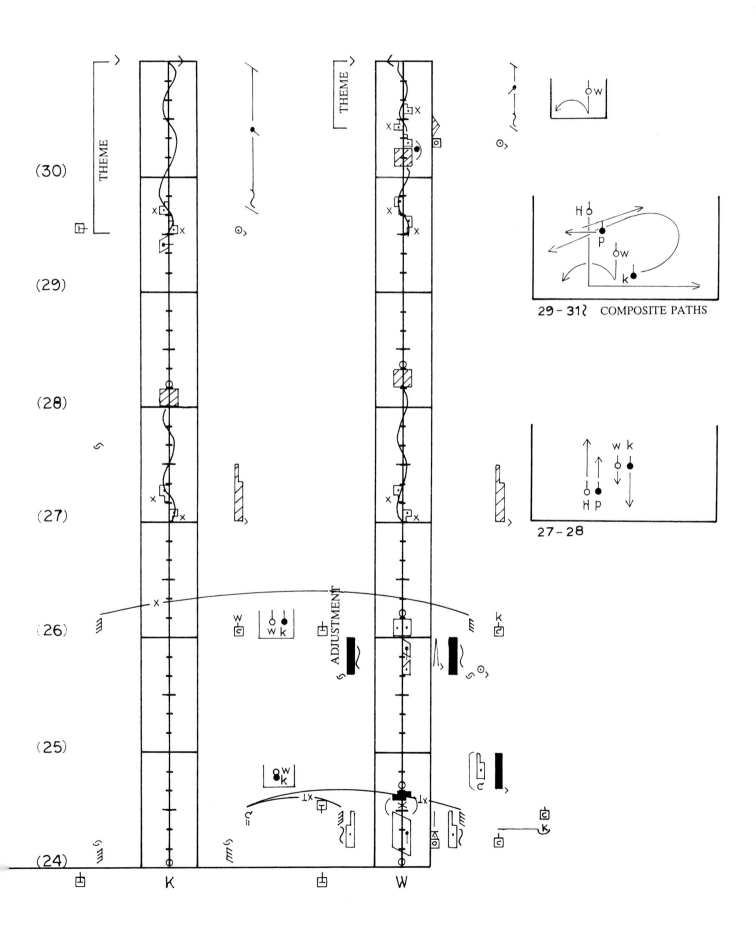

29-31 COMPOSITE PATHS

27-28

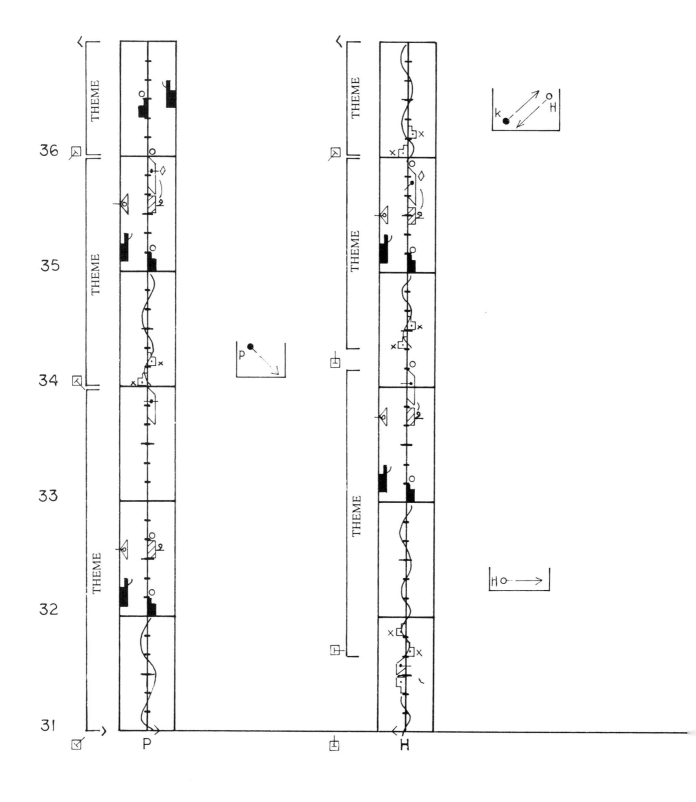

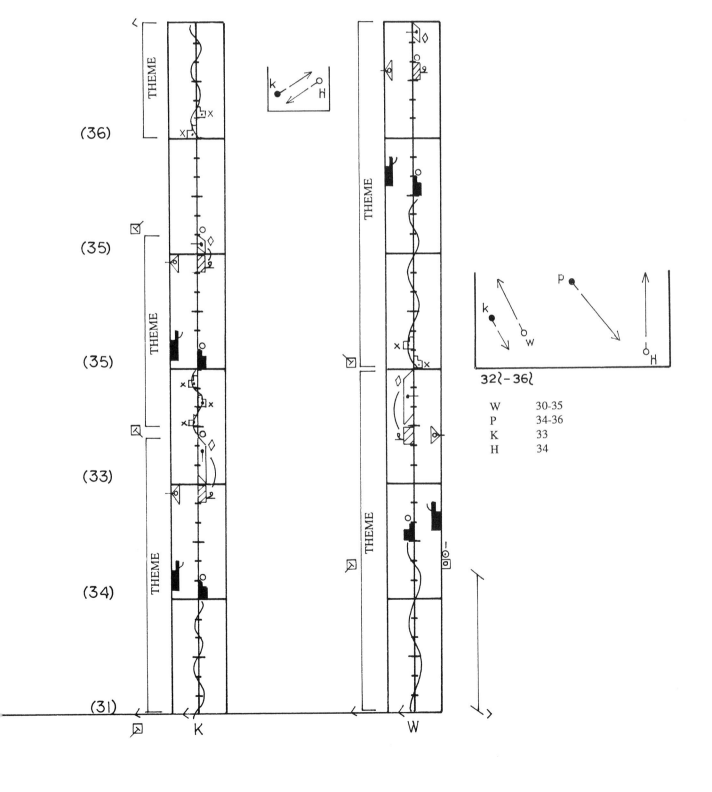

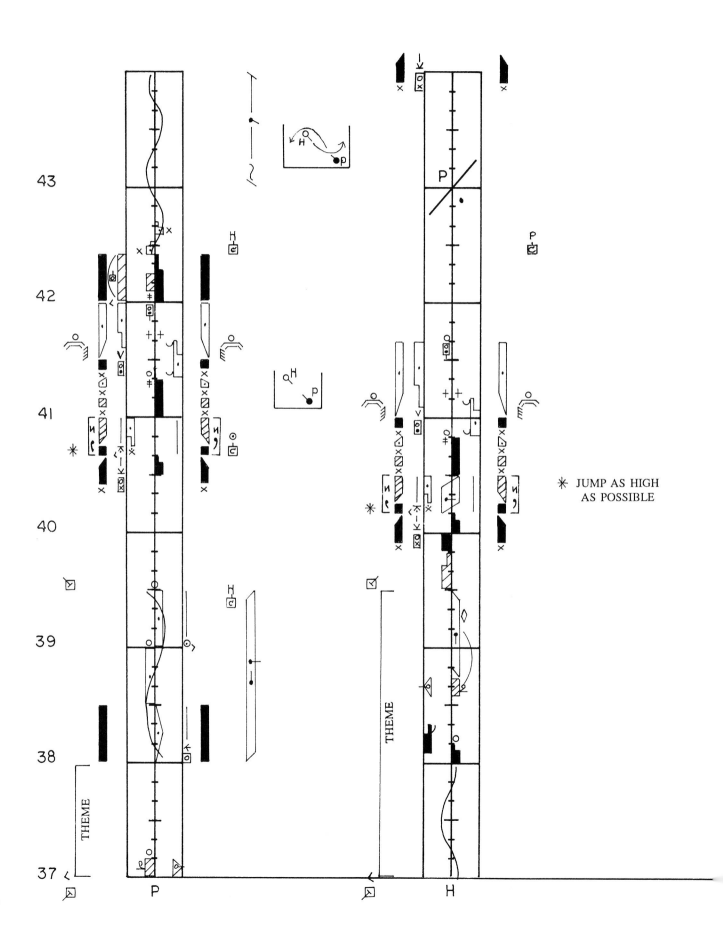

43

42

41

40

39

38

37

* JUMP AS HIGH
   AS POSSIBLE

THEME

THEME

P   H

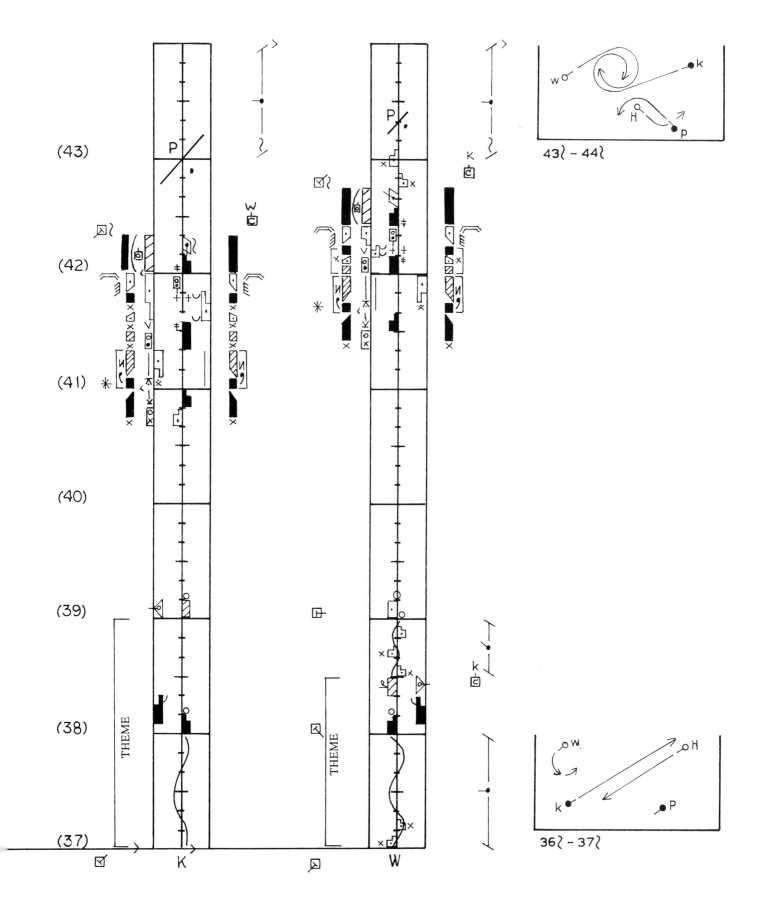

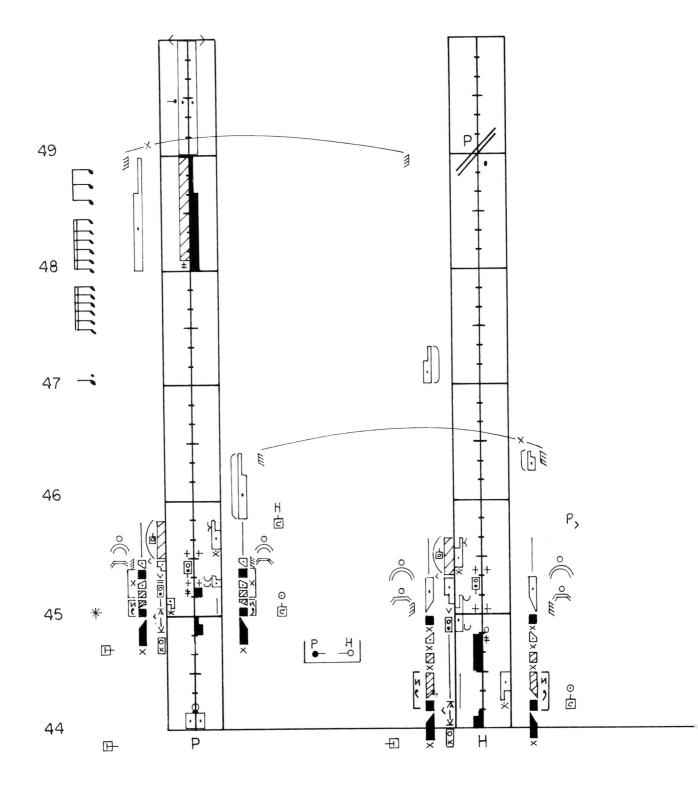

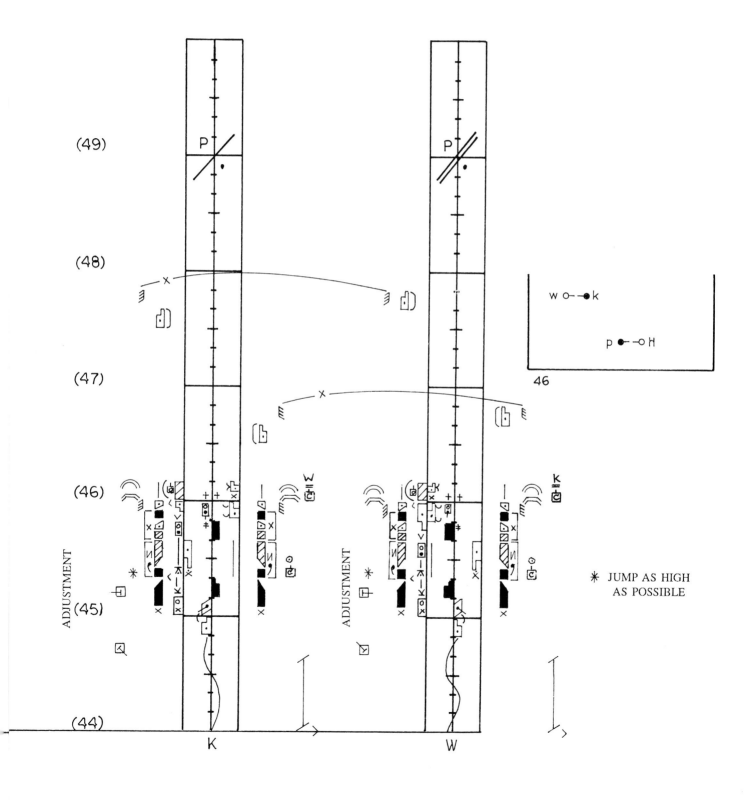

* JUMP AS HIGH
  AS POSSIBLE

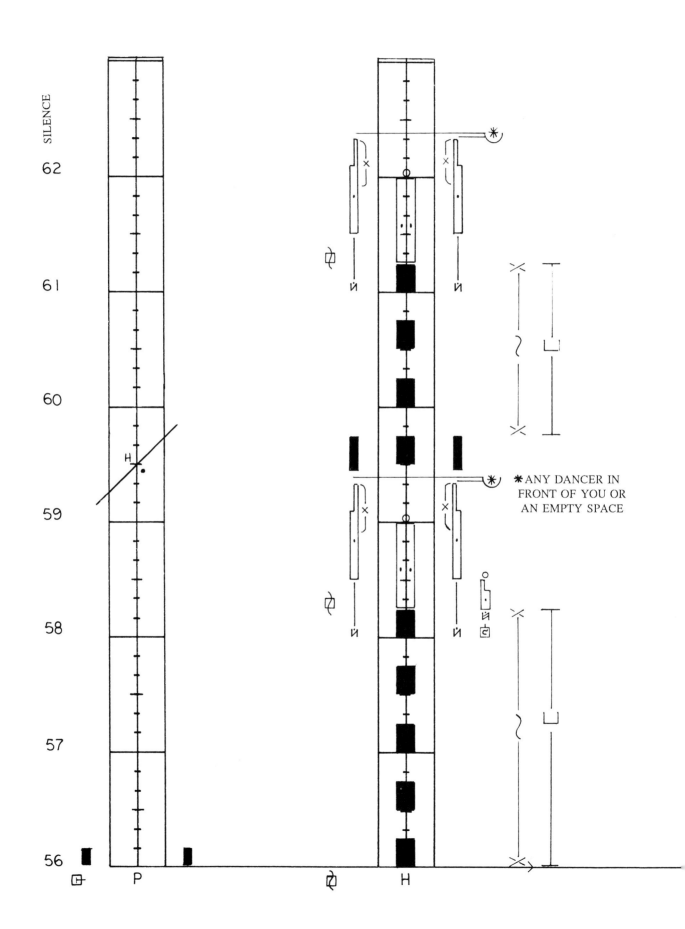

* ANY DANCER IN
FRONT OF YOU OR
AN EMPTY SPACE

KEEP THIS PHRASE GOING IN
SILENCE AS THE CURTAIN COMES IN

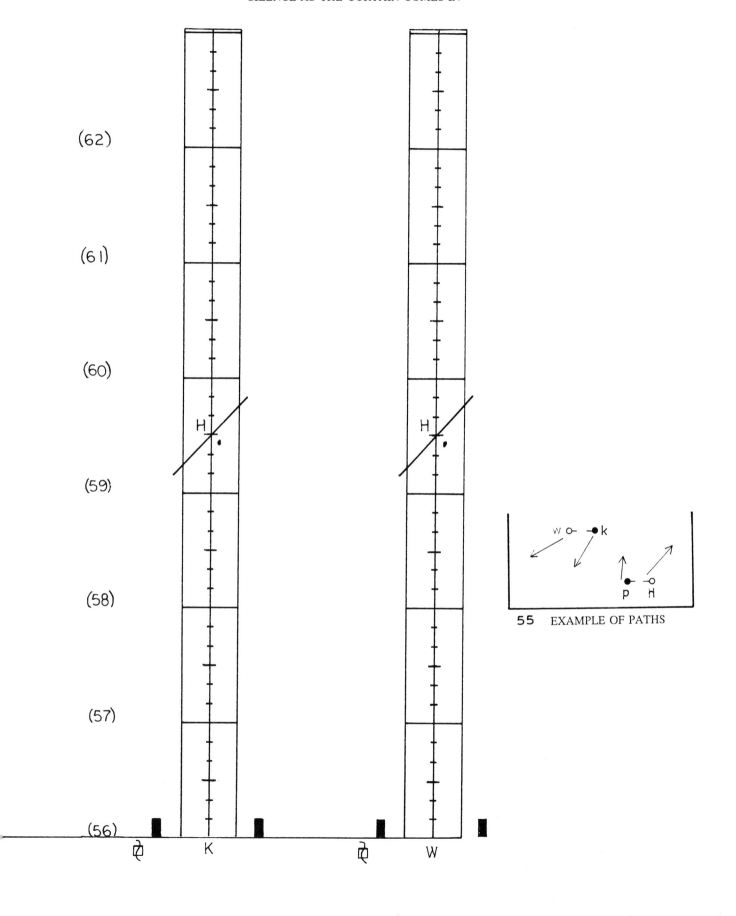

55   EXAMPLE OF PATHS

A TRIBUTE

On July 15 1991 Anna Sokolow received the Samuel H. Scripps American Dance Festival Award at the Page Auditorium of Duke University. The citation read:

"Despite the shifting winds of aesthetic tastes, Miss Sokolow has held true to her beliefs, resolutely teaching the importance of emotional expressiveness, while creating a body of work that combines the power of great drama, the creativity of theatrical vision and the passion of social commitment."

APPENDIX A

Anna Sokolow: A Chronology of Her Artistic Career[1]

The artistic career of Anna Sokolow has spanned sixty years. She has never had a home studio or school such as that enjoyed by Martha Graham, Merce Cunningham, Alwin Nikolais or Alvin Ailey. Her life in dance has been that of a gypsy.

The reader will notice the recurrence of titles in which only the year changes: Opus '58, Opus '63 etc. To keep her finger on the pulse beat of the time, Sokolow updates pieces so that they reflect the music, the popular dance styles (the Twist, the Bossa Nova, Monkey and the Jerk are all given their place at one time or another) and the morals of the times.

As material was collected for this chronology it became apparent that Sokolow may be the most prolific and most travelled of all twentieth century choreographers. Both as an individual artist and as representative of her government she has worked in Australia, Brazil, Canada, Czechoslovakia, England, Germany, Holland, Israel, Japan, Mexico, Poland, Russia, Sweden, Switzerland and Wales. Her work encompasses all forms of theater. On television she has contributed choreography for *Look Up and Live, Lamp Unto My Feet* and *Camera 3*, while an abridged version of *Rooms* was seen on Channel 13. She has also choreographed for the *Perry Como Show* and provided dances for many operas including *Carmen, La Traviata, Die Fledermaus* and *Orpheus in the Underworld.*

On Broadway she worked has alongside Marc Blitzstein, Tennessee Williams, Sidney Howard and Elia Kazan and she was the original choreographer for *Candide* and the musical *Hair* when first produced by Joseph Papp.

Sokolow teaches movement for actors, modern dance technique and choreography. In these capacities she has taught at the Neighborhood Playhouse, the Actor's Studio, American Theater Wing, School of American Ballet, Herbert Berghof School of Acting, Connecticut College School of Dance, Jacob's Pillow, the Juilliard Dance Department and the Juilliard Drama Department, the Swiss Association for Dancers and Gymnasts in Zurich, in Mexico, the Inbal Yemenite Dance Theater and the Habima Theater School in Israel and the dance studio of Mary Anthony in New York City.

In the following chronology each work is placed in the year of its premier. The composer of the music is listed after each title of the work. Note abbreviations: New York City (NYC); Young Men's and Young Women's Hebrew Association (YM-YWHA). Prior to 1945 this organisation was known as Young Men's Hebrew Association (YMHA).

1910   Born Feb. 9th in Hartford Connecticut, the child of Samuel and Sarah (Cohen) Sokolow who had emigrated from Russia - Samuel in 1905/6, Sarah in 1907.

1925   Began intensive modern dance training at the Neighborhood Playhouse. Her teachers were to include Blanche Talmud, Martha Graham and Louis Horst.

1930   Demonstrated in Louis Horst's choreography classes.
Joined the Martha Graham Group, dancing rôles in *Primitive Mysteries* and *Celebrations*. Stayed for eight years.

1933   Her first company, The Dance Unit, presented *Anti-War Trilogy* (later retitled *Anti-War Cycle*), Alexis Soifer. Her first major work sponsored by The Anti-War Congress. (Later to be known as The New Dance League.) At the Grand Street Playhouse, New York City, she presented a solo concert. Works included:
Pre-classic Suite, Soifer
Romantic Dances, Alexander Scriabin
Derision, Serge Prokofiev
Prelude and Choral, César Franck
Histrionics, Paul Hindemith
Salutation to the Morning, Soifer
Jazz Waltz, Louis Gruenberg
Folk Motifs, Béla Bartók/Nicholas Miaskovsky
Homage to Lenin, Miaskovsky

1934   Visited Soviet Union for five months giving solo concerts accompanied by Alex North. John Martin writes in the *New York Times*: *"Of all the young dancers in the field there is none who seems more completely ready to come forth on her own or more likely to make a great career when she finally elects to do so."*
Death of a Tradition, Lopatnikoff, The Workers' Dance League, City Repertory Theater, NYC.
Forces in Opposition, Swift, poem by Sergei Essenin

1935   *American Dance Hall*, Gruenberg
Speaker, Alex North
Strange American Funeral, Elie Siegmeister
Taught dance at YMHA, NYC.
Assisted Louis Horst in production of *Noah,* a play by Obey, Longacre Theater, NYC.

1936   Anna Sokolow and her Dance Unit of the New Dance League at the Theresa L. Kaufmann Auditorium, YMHA, NYC. New works were:
Opening Dance, Vissarion Shebalin
Inquisition '36 - Provocateur, Vigilante, North
Four Little Salon Pieces, Dimitri Shostakovitch
Ballad (in a popular style), North
Suite of Soviet Songs, Lan Adomain
Assisted Martha Graham in directing movement for Theater Guild's production of *Valley Forge*.
Taught during the summer at Triuna Island on Lake George.
Taught dance at the YMHA, NYC.
Gave a joint recital with Lil Liandre at Saratoga Springs.
Participated in the First National Dance Congress and Festival.
Façade, North
Case History No--------, Wallingford Riegger

1937   *War-Monger*, North
        Received one of the first fellowships offered to young artists by the Bennington School
        of Dance.
        Dance Unit of The New Dance League at the Theresa L. Kaufmann Auditorium,
        YMHA, NYC. New works included:
        Excerpts from a War Poem, North, poem by F. T. Martinetti
        Slaughter of the Innocents, North
        Façade - Esposizione Italiana, North, Palmer Auditorium, Bennington College, Vermont
        Invited by John Martin to lecture at the New School, NYC, on "The Revolutionary
        Dance".
        Lecture "Why We Dance and How", Brooklyn Institute of Arts and Sciences, conducted
        by John Martin.
        Taught dance at YMHA, NYC.

1938   With her Dance Unit she makes her modern dance Broadway debut in a concert at the
        Guild Theater, sponsored by the magazine *New Masses.*
        Choreographed pageant *Dance of All Nations* celebrating the 14th anniversary of Lenin's
        death, Madison Square Gardens, NYC.
        Choreographed *Filibuster*, a dance number in the review *The Bourbons Got the Blues* a
        benefit for the National Negro Congress, Mecca Auditorium.
        Appeared as guest artist with Si-lan Chen. Presented by American Friends of the
        Chinese People, Windsor Theater, NYC.
        Appears in a concert for Spain, Hippodrome, NYC.
        Taught dance at the YMHA, NYC.
        Left Martha Graham Dance Company.

1939   *The Exile*, traditional music arranged by North, Alvin Theater, NYC
        Choreographed *The Last Waltz* for the review, *Sing for Your Supper* for the Works
        Progress Administration Project, music Lee Wainer and Ned Lehac, Adelphi Theater,
        NYC but left to prepare for her Mexican tour.
        Invited with her company of twelve, and composer Alex North, by artist Carlos Mérida,
        to give a six-week season at the Palacio de Belles Artes in Mexico City. Stayed to
        teach. With Government backing she starred in the first Mexican modern dance
        company La Paloma Azur (The Blue Dove).
        Danced in the new musical review *America Sings*, New School of Social Research,
        NYC.

1940   Premiered in Mexico: *Los Pies de Pluma*, François Couperin, Girolamo Frescobaldi,
        Johann Mattheson and Jean-Phillipe Rameau
        La Madrugada del Panadero, Rodolfo Halffter
        El Renacuajo Paseador, Silvestre Revueltas
        Entre Sombras Anda el Fuego, Blas Galindo
        Sinfonia de Antigona, Carlos Chavez
        Don Lindo de Almería, Halffter
        Balcon de Espana including sections: *Lluvia de Toros, Caprichiosas, Goyescas, Vision
        Fantastica*, Padre Antonio Soler
        At the YMHA she presented:
        Seven Songs for Children, Revueltas
        Vision Fantastica, Soler
        Prelude, Shostakovitch

1941 *Prelude*, Shostakovitch
      Mill Doors, Max Helfman, poem by Carl Sandburg, NYC
      Mama Beautiful, North, poem by Michael Quinn, NYC
      Homage to Garcia Lorca, which included *Lament for the Death of a Bullfighter* and
      Dance, A Mexican Scene, Revueltas, NYC
      Caprichiosas, Soler, NYC
      Appeared in the American Youth Theater's review *You Can't Sleep Here* at the
      Barbizon Plaza, NYC
1942 *Three Dances to Russian Songs - Cossack Song*, Djerjinsky, *Lullaby*, Alexander
      Gretchaninoff, *Ukrainian Song*, Dunayevsky, Millbrook, NY
      Two Pioneer Marches, Shostakovitch, NYC
      Gave benefit for Russian War Relief, NYC.
1943 At the Theresa L. Kaufmann Auditorium, NYC, *Songs of a Semite*, Richard Neuman
      Madrid 1937, North, YMHA, NYC
1944 *Between the World and Me*, Norman Lloyd, YMHA, NYC
1945 Returned to Mexico. At El Palacio de Belles Artes presented new works:
      Kaddish, Maurice Ravel
      Preludes and Mazurkas, Frederic Chopin
      Concioones Semitas, Hemsi, Carl Engle, Moreno, North
1946 Choreographed dances for Kurt Weill's *Street Scene*, Adelphi Theater, NYC
      The Bride, traditional Jewish folk music, Jordan Hall, Boston
      Danza, Halffter, Jordan Hall, Boston
      At the YM-YWHA she presented:
      Mexican Retable, traditional Mexican folk music
      Two Preludes, Johann Sebastian Bach
      Images from the Old Testament, Hemsi, Engle and folk music
1947 Choreographed *The Great Campaign* by A. Sundgard, North, Princess Theater, NYC.
      Awake Deborah, Hindemith at the Jewish Dance Festival, Hunter College, NYC
      Visited Mexico to teach
      Choreographed for the third evening of "Theater Music of Two Lands", City Center for
      Music and Drama, presented by American-Soviet Music Society.
      Works included:
      A Summer's Day, Prokofiev
      Divertimento, Alexei Haieff
1948 *Life is a Fandango*, Mexican folk music arranged by Robert Didomenica
      Ballad in a Popular Style No. 2, North
      Jewish Dance Festival, Hunter College, NYC
      Choreographed dances for musical *Sleepy Hollow*, George Lessner, Shubert Theatre,
      Philadelphia
      Choreographed dances for review *Small Wonder*, NYC
1949 Choreographed for the Broadway production of Marc Blitzstein's *Regina*, (based on
      Lilian Hellman's *The Little Foxes*), Shubert Theatre, New Haven, Connecticut
      Performed for the Spanish Refugee Appeal, Ziegfeld Theater, NYC
1950 Choreographed musical *Happy as Larry*, M. & W. Porthoff, Coronet Theater, NYC
1951 Gave solo dance concert at Weidman Studio, NYC. Program included solo version of
      The Dybbuk, Siegfried Landau
      Choreographed *A Month of Sundays* for Broadway

1952 *A Short Lecture Demonstration on the Evolution of Ragtime as presented by Jelly Roll Morton*, Jelly Roll Morton, YM-YWHA, NYC

1953 *Lyric Suite*, Alban Berg, Mexico City
Stage movement for Tennessee Williams' *Cameo Real*
Choreographed *City of Angels*, a pageant, Madison Square Garden, NYC.
Invited on the recommendation of Jerome Robbins by the American Fund for Israel (then the Norman Fund) to teach for the Inbal Dance Theater in Israel. Since then she has returned almost every year.
Madam Will You Walk?, musical, Max Marlin, LIN?, Phoenix Theater, NYC
Side Street, North

1954 *Exploration*, Macero, YM-YWHA, NYC
Session for Eight, Macero, YM-YWHA, NYC
L'Histoire du Soldat, Igor Stravinsky, YM-YWHA, NYC

1955 Invited to choreograph for the newly-formed Juilliard Dance Theater directed by Doris Humphrey. Choreographed *Primavera*, A. Benjamin adapted from Domenico Cimarosa.
Choreographed for *Red Roses for Me*, musical, Ewin Finckel, Wilbur Theater, Boston
Rooms, Kenyon Hopkins, YM-YWHA, NYC

1956 Directed *The Moon*, Carl Orff for the New York City Opera
Poem, Scriabin, Brooklyn Academy of Music, Brooklyn
Choreographed *Candide*, Leonard Bernstein, Martin Beck Theater, NYC
Staged dances for New York City Opera Company, *La Traviata, Carmen, Die Fledermaus, The Tempest, Susannah, Orpheus in the Underworld*, New York Center of Music and Drama
Company appeared at The Summer Dance Festival, New London, Connecticut

1957 Staged Franz Kafka's *Metamorphosis*, Hopkins, for a Betty Walburg special matinee performance at the Theatre de Lys, NYC. The production was partly acted, partly mimed and partly danced.
Le Grand Spectacle, Macero, American Ballet Theater experimental program, Phoenix Theater, NYC
Invited to teach at the Juilliard Department of Dance where she has worked ever since.
Staged dances for *Copper and Brass*, David Baker, Martin Beck Theater, NYC

1958 Company performed at the New York Playhouse, NYC
Session for Six, Macero, YM-YWHA, NYC
Opus '58, Macero, Juilliard Dance Ensemble
Lectured on "Dance in Israel" at the YM-YWHA, NYC

1959 Choreograph commission *Three Conversations in a City*, for Perry Como Show, NYC
Three Scriabin Preludes, Scriabin
Choreographed for the opera *Alexander the Hashmonai*, Auldom, Israel Opera House, Tel Aviv

1960 Choreographed dances for the opera *Orfeo*, Christoph Gluck, Mexico
Choreographed *Ester the Queen* for *Lamp Unto My Feet*, R. Starer, Channel 2, NYC
Opus '60, Macero, Palacio de Belles Artes in Mexico City, Mexico
Prepared the Inbal Dance Theater of Israel for their American tour.

1961 *Dreams*, later to become her personal indictment of Nazi Germany, Macero. Later added music by Bach and Anton von Webern, YM-YWHA, NYC
Ofrenda Musical, Bach, Adomian, Palacio de Belles Artes in Mexico City, Mexico
Received 1961 Dance Magazine Award

1962	Invited to assist Elia Kazan by giving movement training for actors of the new Repertory Theater of Lincoln Center
	Founded the Lyric Theater in Tel Aviv, with the help of the American-Israel Foundation, the Rebekah Harkness Foundation, the Lena Robbins Foundation and Rabbi Arthur Lilyveld's Cleveland Ohio Congregation
	Directed *The Treasure*, adapted from a story by J. L. Peretz, Nathan Mishori
	4 Jazz Pieces, Macero, Nachmani Theater, Tel Aviv
	Opus '62, Macero, Tel Aviv, Israel
1963	*Opus '63*, Macero, Juilliard Dance Ensemble
	Conducted a series of lectures at the Herbert Berghof Studio, NYC
	Choreographed *Queen Esther*, Television WCBS
1964	*Odes*, A. U. Boscovitch, Tel Aviv, Israel. Later performed to the music of Edgard Varèse at Juilliard in 1965.
	The Question, Webern, Juilliard Dance Ensemble
	Session for Six, Macero, Juilliard Dance Ensemble
	Forms, Macero, YM-YWHA, NYC
	Taught "Audition Techniques for the Dancer", City College of Performing Arts, NYC
1965	*Ballade*, Scriabin, Juilliard Dance Ensemble
	Opus '65, Macero, Joffrey Ballet apprentice and scholarship students, Delacorte Theater, NYC
	Directed *Bugs* and *Veronica*, two one-act plays both by Johnny White, Macero, Pocket Theater, NYC
1966	*Night*, electronic tape and instruments by Luciano Berio, Juilliard Dance Ensemble
	What's New? Macero, Juilliard Dance Ensemble
	Sokolow Dance Company performed *Dreams* for the visiting Bolshoi Ballet, Brooklyn Academy of Music
	Time + 6, Macero, Boston Ballet Company, Black Bay Theater, Boston
	Invited to teach in Stockholm
1967	Received $10,000 grant from the National Endowment for the Arts and Humanities and premiered at Hunter College, NYC
	Choreographed the award-winning *And the Disciples Departed*, Television WBZ-TV, Boston, Massachusetts
	Deserts, Varèse
	Time + 7, Macero,
	Memories, Macero, Juilliard Dance Ensemble
	Went to Japan on a Fulbright Hays Fellowship to teach at the American Cultural Center
	Taught choreography at the City College for Performing Arts
	Choreographed *The Seven Deadly Sins*, Weill, Netherlands Dance Theater, Holland
	Did the original choreography for *Hair*, The Public Theater, NYC but was fired before opening night
1968	Choreographed *Tribute* as a testimonial to Martin Luther King, Bach, Brooklyn Academy of Music.
	Time plus, Macero, Pennsylvania Ballet Company, Jacob's Pillow, Lee, Massachusetts
	Steps of Silence, Anatol Vieru, Repertory Dance Theater, Salt Lake City, Utah
	Bananas, a burlesque comedy was conceived by Sokolow, directed by John White, presented at The Forum/Vivian Beaumont Theater Building, Lincoln Center, NYC
	Gave lecture demonstration at the YM-YWHA, NYC

1969   *Echoes*, John Weinzweig, Juilliard Dance Ensemble
       Memories revised with music by Tadeusz Baird
       Lectured at Clark Center, NYC
       Formed new company called Lyric Theater
       Act Without Words No. 1, script by Samuel Becket, Joel Thome, Lyric Theater
1970   *Magritte, Magritte*, Scriabin, Franz Liszt, Thome, Eric Satie, Ravel and French songs
       arranged by Virginia Hutchings, with text by John White, Edgar Allen Poe and Paul
       Eluard, Towson State College, Baltimore
       The Dove, Christóbal Halffler, Juilliard Dance Ensemble.
       Lecture demonstration at Dartmouth College
       Choreographed the play *The Dybbuk* for television.
1971   *Scenes from the Music of Charles Ives*, Juilliard Dance Ensemble
       Choreographed dances for *The Merry Wives of Windsor*, American Shakespeare Festival,
       Stratford, Connecticut.
       Metamorphosis, Hopkins, Robert Schumann, Ludwig von Beethoven, Lobe Theater,
       Harvard University, Cambridge, Massachusetts
1972   Toured Holland, Belgium, France and Germany with her new company, Players Project
1973   *In Memory of No. 52436*, Israel
1974   *A Cycle of Cities*, Siegmeister, Wolf Trap Farm Park, Vienna, Virginia
       Come, Come Travel with Dreams, Scriabin, Juilliard Dance Ensemble
       Homage to Federico Garcia Lorca, José Limòn Dance Company, ANTA Theater, NYC
       Ecutorial, Paul Sanasardo Dance Company, Brooklyn Academy of Music
       Quartertones, Ives, American Theater Laboratory, NYC
       Lectured on "Dance in Israel", YM-YWHA, NYC
       Received Creative Arts Award, Brandeis University
1975   *Ride the Cultural Loop*, Macero, Juilliard Dance Ensemble
       Moods, G. Ligeti, Contemporary Dance System, The American Place Theater, NYC
       Contemporary Dance System presents a tribute to Anna Sokolow, American Place
       Theater, NYC
1976   Subject of a film biography *They Are Their Own Gifts* by Margaret Murphy and Lucille
       Rhodes, NYC
       Ellis Island, poem by Emma Lazarus, Ives, Juilliard Dance Ensemble
1977   *Homage to Alexander Scriabin*, Scriabin, Contemporary Dance System, Amherst
       College, Amherst, Massachusetts
       The Holy Place, Ernest Bloch, Juilliard Dance Ensemble
1978   *Songs Remembered*, David Diamond, Juilliard Dance Ensemble
       Poe, stage play, Chopin, Marianna Rosett, Rachmaninoff, Juilliard Drama Department
       Asi es la Vida en Mexico, Revueltas, Juilliard Dance Ensemble
       Received Honary Doctorate, University of Ohio
       Homage to Gertrude Kraus, Ravel, Israel
1979   *Opus '79*, Macero, Chicago
       Homage to Scriabin, solo, Scriabin, Camera Mart, Stage One, NYC
       Wings, Mark Kopitman, text Israel Eliraz
       La Noche de los Mayas, Mecado, Baile, Procession, Juilliard Dance Theater
1980   Speaker/choreographer for Memorial Program honoring Fred Berk, YM-YWHA, NYC
       From the Diaries of Franz Kafka, play, Schumann, Gustav Mahler, Arnold Schoenberg
       and Jewish Liturgical music, Juilliard Theater Center

1981   Reformed company, New Players' Project, an eight-member ensemble and premiered at
       the Abraham Goodman House in Manhattan
       Song of Songs, Neuman, Abraham Goodman House, NYC
       Song of Deborah, Bach, Abraham Goodman House, NYC
       Los Conversas, Neuman, Juilliard Dance Ensemble
1982   *Elegy*, Mahler, Mary Anthony Dance Theater, Marymont Theater, NYC
       Everything Must Go, Macero, Juilliard Dance Ensemble
       Les Noces, Stravinsky, Batsheva Dance Company, Israel
       Choreographed *Mikhoels the Wise*, opera, Bruce Adolphe, YM-YWHA, NYC
       Kafka, Merkin Mall, NYC
1983   Directed and choreographed *Hanna* (revision of *Wings* 1979), Harold Clurman Theater,
       NYC
       Four Preludes, Rachmaninoff, Juilliard Dance Ensemble
       Transfigured Night, Schoenberg, Eleo Pamare Dance Company, Joyce Theater, NYC
       Piano Preludes, George Gershwin, Players' Project
1984   *Lament for Death of a Bullfighter*, Revueltas
       Ballad in a Popular Style, Chick Corea
       Kaddish, Ravel, Riverside Church, NYC
1985   *One Who Cared: A Homage to Janusz Korchak*, a dance-drama, libretto Matti Megged,
       Thome, Carnegie-Mellon University, Pittsburgh
       Choreographs in London and Dublin
1986   National Foundation for Jewish Culture honored Sokolow at a gala benefit at the Joyce
       Theater, NYC
1987   Visiting lecturer in the Performing Arts at Harvard University
       Two Preludes, Rachmaninoff, Riverside Church, NYC
       Golda Meir: Ideals and Dreams, Thome, Gusman Theater for the Performing Arts,
       Miami, Florida
1988   *Kurt Weill*, YM-YWHA, NYC
       Stations of the Cross, Marcel Dupré, Juilliard Dance Ensemble, St. Bartholomew's
       Episcopal Church, NYC
1989   *Rooms*, Hopkins, Berlin Opera House, Germany
       Players' Project performed in Taiwan
1990   Israel celebrated her 80th birthday by planting 350 trees in her honor
       Taught choreography YM-YWHA, NYC
1991   YM-YWHA celebrated her 81st birthday
       Received the Samuel H. Scripps American Dance Festival Award

1. See also the recently published biography of Anna Sokolow by Larry Warren, published in 1991 by Princeton Book
Company, Princeton, NJ, USA.

APPENDIX B

Sokolow Works Recorded in Labanotation

TITLE	MUSIC	NOTATOR
Ballade: Quartet Version	Alexander Scriabin	Ray Cook 1974[1]
Sextet Version		Ray Cook 1974
Deserts	Edgard Varèse	Ray Cook 1979
Dreams	Bach/Webern/Macero	Ray Cook 1974
Ellis Island, "Women's Dance"	Charles Ives	Kathy Tirrill 1976
The Holy Place, "Couples Section"	Ernest Bloch	Teresa Coker 1977
Homage to Scriabin	Alexander Scriabin	Ray Cook 1977
Kaddish	Maurice Ravel	Lynne Weber 1974
Lyric Suite	Alban Berg	Ray Cook 1972
Magritte, Magritte	Scriabin/Liszt/Finch/French Music Hall Ballads	Ilene Fox 1982
Moods	György Ligeti	Ray Cook assisted by Charlotte Wile 1975
Night	Luciano Berio	Colette Yglesias Leslie Brown 1973
Odes: Duet	Edgard Varèse	Muriel Topaz, 1965
Opus '63, (Third & Fourth Movements)	Teo Macero	Ray Cook Martha Clark 1963
Poe	Druckman/Roldan/Harrison /Chopin	Jane Marriett 1977

TITLE	MUSIC	NOTATOR
Quartertones	Charles Ives	Lynne Weber 1974
Ride the Cultural Loop, "Sections from Puerto Rico; East; Average Couples"	Teo Macero	Holly Stern, Mary Ann Golick, Nancy Hill, Rosemary Newton 1975
Rooms	Kenyon Hopkins	Ray Cook 1967 & 1972-75
Scenes from the Music of Charles Ives	Charles Ives	Ilene Fox 1983-84
Session for Six	Teo Macero	Muriel Topaz 1965
A Short Lecture and Demonstration on the Evolution of Ragtime as Demonstrated by Jelly Roll Morton	Jelly Roll Morton	Muriel Topaz 1972
Steps of Silence	Anatol Vieru	Ray Cook 1975
Three Poems, "Section One"	Joel Thom	Debbie Zalkind, Nancy Mapother 1973

1. The date given is the date of the notation and not the date of the premier.

APPENDIX C

Notes on Music

The Selected Scriabin Pieces

The dance is choreographed in sections and the music for each section is as follows:

OPENING   Opus 11 No. 1   Start at [13] and play to the end, then play from beginning to end.

OPENING CONTINUED   Opus 15 No. 2

QUARTET   Opus 11 No. 11

WOMAN'S SOLO   Opus 11 No. 10

POEM - TWO DUETS   Opus 32 No. 1

MAN'S SOLO   Opus 42, No. 1 in D Flat Minor

ENDING   Opus 59 No. 2

Setting

The music should be played with the piano on stage, on the downstage left apron. The pianist must be included in the dance scene.

Cues

The pianist will cue from the dancer at the following measures:

> **Opening** - - - - - measure 15
> **Opening Continued** - measure 9
> **Woman's Solo** - - - measure 1
> **Poem - Two Duets** - measures 1 and 15

APPENDIX D

THE MUSIC SCORE

1) In the autograph MS and in Belyaev's edition:

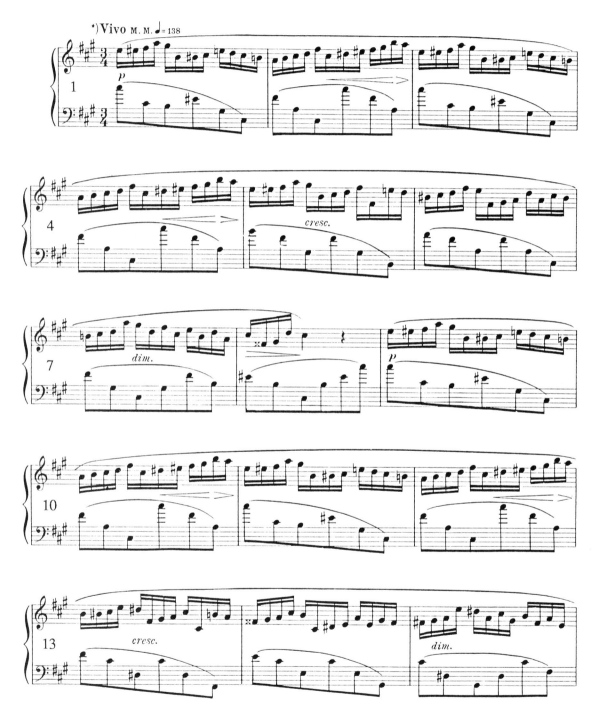

* Scriabin originally wrote *Agitato*. Later this was deleted and replaced by *Vivo*.

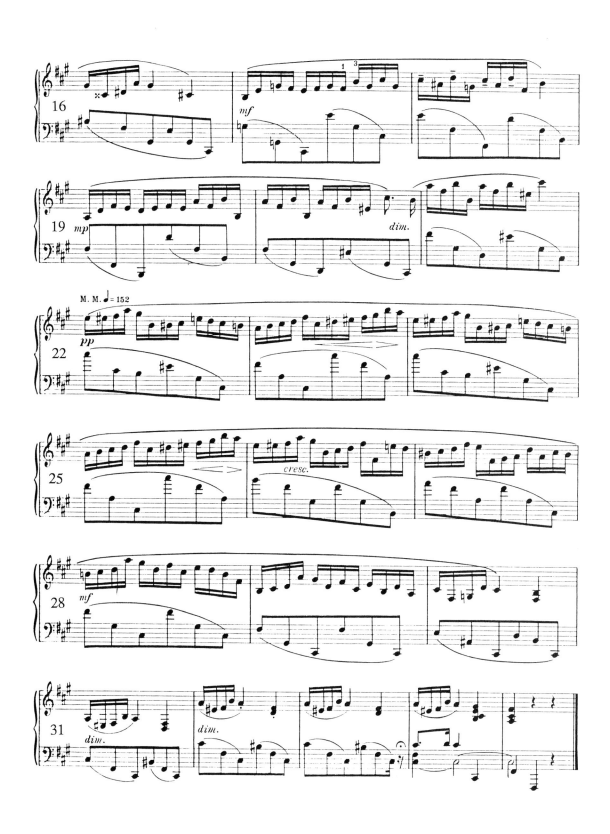

1) *rit.* (according to the composer's instructions).

1) The MS here has a *rit.* leading to a slower tempo: starting with the third measure of this line,
♩.♩♪=100 (in accordance with the MS).

2) According to the composer's instructions, a brief caesura with following *p* is possible
before the g sharp.